INTERPRETATIONS

INTERPRETATIONS

By
L. COPE CORNFORD

KENNIKAT PRESS
Port Washington, N. Y./London

INTERPRETATIONS

First published in 1926
Reissued in 1970 by Kennikat Press
Library of Congress Catalog Card No: 77-105773
ISBN 0-8046-0945-4

Manufactured by Taylor Publishing Company   Dallas, Texas

PREFACE

TO the diversity of the subjects with which the following essays are concerned the kind reader will I hope be reconciled by a certain unity in their treatment. Life itself is a series of diverse and surprising manifestations, observing no visible method in the order of their appearance; yet each and all, challenging fortitude, or inviting curiosity, or proffering delight, demand response; and as it is by the quality of their response men shape their destiny, so it would seem that the attempt to interpret the meaning, alike of demand and response, may have its uses, although serving only to entertain a few moments' leisure.

The substance of some of these essays appeared in *The Morning Post*, *The National Review*, and *The Christian Science Monitor*, to whose proprietors the author desires to make his acknowledgments.

L. C. C.

CONTENTS

I: PERSONS

(1)

(2)

II: BOOKS

INTERPRETATIONS

III: THREE SKETCHES

IV: THE FIRST ANNIVERSARY

V: THE NAVY TRIUMPHANT

I: *PERSONS* (1)

LORD CHARLES BERESFORD

(*ADMIRAL LORD BERESFORD OF METEMMEH*, *G.C.B.*, *G.C.V.O.*, *LL.D.*, *D.C.L.*)

(1846–1919)

ഗ

THERE are two Englands. One is of the
sea and the other of the land. Admiral
Lord Beresford is, perhaps, the only great
seaman who toiled and fought, commanded men
and directed affairs, and took his pleasures in both
hemispheres. And here we touch at once the
tragedy of his life. Supreme at sea, he brought
the tradition of the sea and the seaman's code
of honour into the civilian turmoil of warring
ambitions, and although he was never defeated
(being undefeatable) he was overwhelmed. For
the tradition of the sea is, first and last, loyalty ;
it is compact of an absolute sincerity, the strict
fulfilment of duty because it is duty, swift decision and resolute action. And the seaman's code
of honour is the code of chivalry, which is the
principle of service, and which survives in the
fighting Services and in the Churches. In Beresford's youth, the ideal of public service was still
acknowledged among the rulers of England ; he
lived to see it perish, and that was a thing he could
never understand. He dealt with authority in
high places on the assumption that he was dealing with honourable men ; and when he found he

was mistaken, what course was left open to him? Clearly none. The ways of the new men were not his ways; their thoughts were not his thoughts; and of using their weapons he was merely incapable.

Beresford first entered Parliament in 1874, as Member for Waterford, after a really glorious Irish election, old style. One night he was stoned in the dark. He relates the incident in his *Memoirs*[1]: "A large missile caught me behind the ear, knocking me over. Next morning I related the incident to one of my most enthusiastic supporters in the place. ' 'Tis a disgrace,' said I, ' throwing stones in the dark. And as for that boy who made a good shot, if I could get hold of him I would scatter his features.' ' Ye would not,' said he. ' And why wouldn't I?' said I. ' Because,' says he, ' it was meself threw that brick. An' didn't I get ye grand,' says he. ' But ye're not hurted. Sure ye're not hurted, or I wouldn't have told ye annything about it.' " Well, well. A few months before his death, Lord Beresford suffered from an effusion of blood at the base of the skull, at the spot, as he told the present writer, upon which the stone struck him in 1874.

Beresford was returned in the Conservative interest. During the first debate to which he listened, he became convinced that the Opposition speaker was right. "That is the only man who has solved the difficulty, and if he divides I shall vote with him," said Lord Charles Beresford, M.P.

[1] *The Memoirs of Lord Charles Beresford* (London, Methuen).

14

And he recalls that "my innocent remark was received with a volley of expostulations. I was told that I had only just joined political life, and that I did not understand it; that the Radical speaker's plan was excellent, but that the other side could not be allowed to take the credit of producing a good scheme, because it would do our side harm in the country; that the scheme would be thrown out for the time, in order that our side might be able, later on, to bring in the same scheme and reap the credit of it, and so forth. ' Well,' I said, ' if this kind of tactics is required in politics, it is no place for me. I had better go back to sea.' Whereupon I was told that I should shake down to political methods when I had been a year or two in the House. But I have spent years in politics, and I have never shaken down to political methods. A thing is either right or wrong. I have never scrupled to vote against my own party when I thought they were in the wrong."

That simple confession of faith was absolutely sincere. How could such a man attain to political place and power? Beresford would have liked both place and power, loving, as he did, action before all things else; but he would not step an inch aside to get them; and what chance had he compared with men whose whole energy was absorbed in achieving their personal ambitions? Beresford desired neither rank nor wealth. There are few noble families in the United Kingdom bearing more distinguished quarterings than the Beresfords of Curraghmore; and as for money, Beresford seldom knew whether he had any or not. He thought that money is for spending. His habit, in his earlier years, was to leave details of finance to his servant and his banker, keeping one sovereign in his pocket for emergencies, and usually giving it away.

Beresford was not two men, one of the sea and the other of the shore. He was one and the same, and all of a piece. But when he came on shore, people saw only Charlie Beresford, the beloved of the populace, who adored a sportsman. When he was driving the Heir to the Throne in his tandem, some one shouted : " 'Ullo, Charlie, is that Wales you've got beside you ? " They saw only the Beresford who rode a pig down Park Lane at sunrise on his way back from a dance ; who ran a hundred yards race with another Irish lord at a Royal garden-party and beat him ; who habitually rode in steeplechases ; who carried away a toll-gate on the back of his trap into Plymouth, because the toll-keeper refused to open it ; who tamed and trained an elephant on board H.M.S. *Galatea* ; and who, with his brother, cut the too-long locks of the porter at Limerick Junction with the snuffers of the station lamps, and, " ' Sure,' said the porter, ' I'll grow my hair again as quick as I can the way you'll be giving me another tip ' " ; who, when he was flag-lieutenant at Plymouth, had seated the whole Board of Admiralty in his coach in order to drive the Lords Commissioners down to witness naval manœuvres, when Rear-Admiral Beauchamp Seymour interfered with the party.

" ' You don't know that boy,' said Seymour. ' He's not safe ! He'll upset you on purpose just to say he's upset the whole Board of Admiralty.' " The worthy Admiral, afterwards Lord Alcester, famed for his bombardment of Alexandria and his good dinners, unconsciously revealed the official mind, as it was then, is now, and will be for ever. It is afraid of being upset.

But society on shore, smiling pleasantly at the reckless, gallant, hard-riding, witty, and inextinguishably gay young Irish aristocrat, had no notion of the naval officer at sea. Charles Beresford entered the Old Navy of masts and sails at thirteen : the Old Navy of immense sporting cruises all round the world, of terrific discipline, of fierce joviality, of a superb seamanship unmatched in the world. Beresford's account, in his *Memoirs*, of H.M.S. *Marlborough* is one of the most vivid pictures of the old Victorian Navy ever limned.

" What can be more glorious," writes Beresford, " than a ship getting under way ? She quivers like a sentient thing amid the whole moving, tumultuous, lusty life. Men are racing aloft ; other men, their feet pounding upon the white decks, are running away with the ropes ; the ringing commands and the shouting fill the air ; the wind strikes with a salt and hearty sting ; and the proud and beautiful creature rises to the lift of the sea. Doctors, paymasters, idlers and all used to run up on deck to witness that magnificent spectacle, a full-rigged ship getting under sail."

During the voyage, whose beginning he thus sketches, Beresford, then a midshipman, saved the ship from driving dead on shore in a hurricane, perceiving the danger just in time. It was then he first heard the boatswain's pipe crying "*Save ship*." He heard that desperate melody once again, off the west coast of North America, in a full gale. Before he was promoted to lieutenant, Beresford had served a commission in the Mediterranean; sailed round the Horn; shot geese in the Falkland Islands; helped to bring to Panama Queen Emma of the Sandwich Islands; cut the first trail through the virgin forest of Vancouver; learned seamanship in every detail, down to cutting out sails, under Captain Lord Gillford; helped to extinguish a great fire in Valparaiso, and had seen one of the first submarines leave the coast of Chile and sink never to rise. As lieutenant, Beresford sailed in H.M.S. *Galatea* with the Duke of Edinburgh, and visited Cape Town, Australia, New Zealand, Tahiti, the Sandwich Islands, Japan, China, India, and the Falkland Islands.

When he entered Parliament Beresford was twenty-eight years old, and had been fifteen years in the Navy, of which period he spent the greater part at sea. A photograph shows a handsome youth with crisp curly hair, already worn away from the forehead by the pressure of his uniform cap, with the unmistakable sheathed, alert gaze of the seaman, and kindly, humorous mouth. That cheery youth had crammed into fifteen years more exploits, hardships, adventures, and experiences

18

than most of his friends in Parliament achieved in the whole of their lives. But they knew nothing of the education of the sea. To society, the sea was (and is) merely the Beyond, wherein a few eccentric persons unaccountably roved in the intervals of living in the real world. People only know what they have seen. So they never understood Charles Beresford. But the lad was only beginning. Of magnificent physique, abounding energy, and irresistible spirits, life was his adventure, a great big splendid playground, in which hard knocks, given and taken, were all part of the game.

He fought at Alexandria, as all the world knows ; and Lieutenant the Hon. Hedworth Lambton suggested to the Admiral, Sir Beauchamp Seymour (he who had said, " You don't know that boy. He's not safe ! "), that the signal should be made, " Well done, *Condor*." Hedworth Lambton, afterwards Admiral of the Fleet the Hon. Sir Hedworth Meux, lived to be Beresford's pallbearer. But, as all the world does not know, this young commander of thirty-six was appointed Provost-Marshal and Chief of Police to restore order in Alexandria. Here was a business demanding, above all, ability of organization, tact, and resolution. Beresford had the whole town as orderly as Regent Street, and everybody pleased, inside a fortnight. He saved Alexandria from being burned to the ground, saved hundreds of lives and millions' worth of property. In the Sudan War of 1884–85, Beresford organized the hauling of the boats for the Nile Expedition through the roaring cataracts of the Bab-el-Kebir, a consummate feat of seamanship; and subsequently he commanded the Naval Brigade. Beresford marched across the desert in the expedition sent (too late) to rescue Gordon; fought at Abu Klea; fought three thousand Dervishes in the little river-steamer *Safieh*, and so saved both Sir Charles Wilson and his party, and, by delaying the whole Dervish advance, saved the River Column. He afterwards saved it again by giving General Sir Redvers Buller a timely piece of advice.

Beresford had proved himself to be a born leader of men, with an extraordinary comprehension of the nature of war. His sole reward was the approbation of Queen Victoria, who, as she pinned the C.B. to his coat, said : " I am very pleased with you." Not so the Lords Commissioners of the Admiralty, who refused to count Beresford's three hundred and fifteen days in the Sudan either as war service or as part of the sea-time necessary for promotion.

Beresford came home to do two things. One was to establish a War Staff at the Admiralty ; the other was to strengthen the Navy in accordance with the plan to be devised by the War Staff. He did both, and in so doing he sacrificed his career. He established an Intelligence Department, under Captain William H. Hall (father of Vice-Admiral Sir William R. Hall, M.P., Director of Naval Intelligence during the War), which the authorities stubbornly declined to develop into a

War Staff until the middle of the War of 1914-
1918. He forced the Government to vote twenty-
one millions to increase the Navy in accordance
with his own and Captain Hall's estimate of
requirements. Beresford resigned his post at the
Admiralty in order to compel public attention to
the dangers of the position, and he was never
again employed at the Admiralty.

Perhaps Beresford, in resigning, made a mistake. In such a position an honest man must
consider that, if he resigns, he will probably
achieve his object, but that he will certainly ruin
his career, for the official mind never forgives; and
that if he does not resign, it is still possible that
he may achieve his object and save his career as
well. Beresford took what he believed to be the
honourable course.

Now, if the Admiralty and the Government,
then consisting of public-spirited men generally
desirous, in their various degrees, to do the right
thing, had understood what Beresford had done
in the Egyptian War, what was his achievement as
a seaman, and what was the quality of his mind,
it is possible that they would have followed his
counsel. But they did not know, and they did not
perceive, these things. Beresford was the last man
to tell them. Or, if Beresford had assumed importance, put on the official solemnity, pretended
a holy deference to authority, and conducted an
elaborate diplomatic intrigue in the approved
manner, they might have understood. But Beresford was utterly incapable even of conceiving the

notion. The official airs of authority struck him as comic. For subterfuge he had a profound contempt. He met solemnity with a jest, and struck out at opposition. It was of no use to try to humbug Beresford. He simply told you that you were a liar. It was dangerous to threaten him, because he would pitch you out of the window. To bribe him was impossible. For one thing, the man wanted nothing, and for another, he had his own views on that subject. It only remained to concede to him what he demanded, steal the credit of it, and then proceed to wear him down until he could give no more trouble. And that is what happened.

There is, or was, a theory that the Powers-that-be, Ministers, great officials, Departments, Boards, Committees, and the whole constellation in general, although they may, and do, make occasional mistakes, are inspired by a conscientious desire to do the best for the country, so that they are habitually watching to discover new ideas and new men able to carry those ideas into execution. The conception is partly true and partly false, because the Powers-that-be consist of individuals, and some of them are honest men, and some of them are clever men, and some are both honest and clever, while others, as the Frenchman said, are not so good. But the Powers-that-be must hold together, for that is the condition of their existence. When they meet with one who, while acknowledging the just claims of Authority, is still constitutionally incapable of believing in the divine right of Authority, the Powers-that-be instinctively distrust that irreverent person. He knows too much. According to the conventional theory, when Beresford demanded the creation of a War Staff, or thinking department, which should define the requirements of national defence in accordance with the policy of the Government, the authorities should have received his proposals with gratitude and praise, and should instantly have endowed him with full discretion to carry his plan into execution. For his plan both secured national safety and economized force and money. But what actually happened was that a part of Beresford's scheme was adopted under compulsion, and that afterwards Authority gradually undid his work.

What was Beresford's proposal? "What my friends used to call my 'craze,'" he writes, "which they regarded as an amiable form of lunacy, for organization for war, showed me that without it all naval force, though it were twice as powerful, would be practically wasted in the event of emergency. . . . That there existed no department charged with the duty of constantly representing what was required in ships, men, stores, docks, under peace conditions, or what would be required under war conditions, was obvious enough. But in the course of the execution of my duties as Junior Lord (in 1886), it immediately became equally clear that the Navy was deficient in those very matters and things concerning which it would have been the business of such a department to report. Among them was coal, which was in my charge. Not only was there an immense deficiency in the war reserve of coal, but there was no plan for supplying it."

What Beresford proposed was, that there should be formed at the Admiralty a department charged with the collection of information, upon which could be based the requirements of the Fleet. Thus, the increase or decrease of foreign navies, the changes of international polities, the alterations of British policy, the exact condition of the British Fleet and its distribution, would be noted from day to day. Not until such information was collected could the authorities estimate what should be the strength of the Fleet, now and in the future. Thence arose the further consideration, that the required strength and disposition of the Fleet depended upon what it was required to do in the event of war with this Power or that. From which necessity arose the further necessity for creating a department charged with the duty of making plans for war. That is what is meant by a War Staff. The institution of the Intelligence Department was thus intended to be the preliminary to the institution of the War Staff.

The system is so simple and so sensible that people who do not understand the official mind are at a loss to understand why it did not exist, and still less why, when it was suggested, it was opposed. The full explanation is lucidly presented by Lord Beresford in his *Memoirs*. In this place it must suffice to say the system was in fact the system followed in the Nelsonic era ; that it fell into disuse in the years of peace ; and that it was actually put into practice by the late Admiral of the Fleet Sir Frederick Richards, First Sea Lord, when, with his colleagues, he planned the great naval defence scheme of 1893, whose execution kept the peace of Europe at the time of the Fashoda incident and until 1914. Guided by Sir Frederick Richards, the Board of Admiralty served as a War Staff, and that noble seaman's genius and determination enabled him to do the work which, owing to the vast increase of the responsibilities of the Navy, can no longer be accomplished by one man. It should be added that the idea of a War Staff was presented in 1884 and subsequently by various lay students of the subject, among whom Professor Spenser Wilkinson performed valuable public service.

When it came to the supreme test of war, it presently became evident that, unless a proper executive War Staff was constituted at the Admiralty, this country—not to put too fine a point upon it— would be defeated. Then, and not until then, at the price of prolonging the war for two years, did Authority, under the lash of necessity, do what Beresford had proved to be essential thirty years before.

This, then, is a part of the heritage Beresford has bequeathed to his country. Another part is less tangible, but not less enduring. During his years in command afloat, Beresford had trained in war the admirals and captains who served in the Grand Fleet.

The Grand Fleet itself was constituted by Beresford, inasmuch as he succeeded in convincing the Asquith administration of the instant necessity for forming a single large homogeneous fleet complete in all units. Beresford specified in what those units should consist, and in every particular in which the Liberal Government chose to ignore his counsel, they were forced in time of war to repair their criminal neglect at a cost of millions to the country. Various persons are still swaggering about saying they did all these things. Beresford said nothing. He saved others; and they took care he should suffer thereby. The most of his friends were content to stand by and shake their heads over the rashness of poor Charlie Beresford.

Nevertheless, Charles Beresford had the brain of a statesman. There was no shrewder judge of men; none better qualified to deal with affairs. For one of Beresford's shining virtues was his perfect fearlessness in facing facts. It is a seaman's quality; for in a gale of wind it is no use pretending. The penalty of moral cowardice at sea is simply death. But it is another quality of the seaman that his action is decisive, open, and aboveboard. Beresford rode as straight in politics as in the hunting field. But that is not the way of the politicians, nor the path of diplomacy. Beresford lacked the peculiar gift which brings men of mediocre endowment to occupy high positions.

At sea, where the air is clean and an honourable tradition rules, Beresford was superb. He commanded the entire confidence and the personal affection of officers and men. And above all, he owned, what perhaps no other seaman has possessed since Nelson, the extraordinary gift of intuition. *He knew what the enemy was going to do next*, and he also knew what to do to defeat the enemy. An officer of his staff in his flagship told the present writer that one night, in the middle of manœuvres, Beresford suddenly ordered the entire fleet to go about. The whole of his staff were smitten with consternation. After days of elaborate calculation, the Admiral made a signal which upset everything, and they were ready to burst into tears. Beresford was imperturbable as usual. " I know what the other fellows are doing," he said, " and we'll be there first." *And he was right.* Here, in a word, was a man endowed with the supreme, the unique gift of leadership, the touch of genius which no study nor art nor labour can attain ; and Authority pushed him aside, derided him, wasted him.

When war came, Beresford volunteered his services. They were refused. But Beresford had no thought of himself. He was thinking of his country. There can be no harm now in recording that in friendly conversation with Cabinet Ministers, Beresford, with his perfect equanimity and swift intuition, suggested what should be done, and done at once, for the defence of ports, harbours, and arsenals, and for the protection of merchant ships. He understood, as very few understood, the peril of the situation. Then it was that Government and public alike believed the war would be quickly ended. Not so Beresford. "You think you can put the German Empire on its back in six months?" he said. "You are mistaken."

With his vast knowledge and his incomparable experience, perceiving what ought to be done and debarred from action, Beresford sat down to keep the accounts of war charities and to write letters, working for many hours a day. Every one in need came to him for help. Naval ratings with a grievance, widows of naval men, old shipmates; these had been his constant care for years, and every appeal was answered with punctilious courtesy, and many a poor man's trouble was righted. Now, in addition, Beresford dealt with the organizations for supplying comforts to the Fleet, and with great sums of money subscribed for like purposes.

Labouring thus patiently in his study, day after day, denying himself even his daily ride, Beresford served his country to the last. Alert, indomitable, and cheery as ever, accessible to all, scrupulously punctual in every engagement, he drudged from early morn till late at night; while the Fleet— *his* Fleet—keeping the sea under the most appalling difficulties, lacked him. While the tide of battle rolled along three hundred miles of the Western Front, the veteran who fought in the square at Abu Klea, who marched with the forlorn hope across the desert, who held up an army in a paddle-steamer, saved the River Column, marched with Buller in the retreat, and saved the River

Column again, was left aside. He was an old man, as years go, but age had scarce diminished his magnificent strength nor shadowed his inimitable brilliance. His sturdy figure, of the true seaman's build, short, deep-chested, muscular, stood like a tower. The years had rounded his face and whitened his hair, so that he looked benign as a bishop. But in the clear blue eyes, shrewd and kindly, the lids drawn down upon the corners, with their glance as of one who habitually scanned sea-distances, beamed the man's unquenchable and noble spirit.

To know Charles Beresford was to love him. Even the prudent, whom he embarrassed, held him in affection and a secret admiration. As for the people, they worshipped him. An aristocrat of the most democratic country in the world, Beresford conversed on equal terms with all men. But the people followed him because they knew him to be straight and honest, outspoken and utterly fearless, of an abounding kindness of heart, a notable fighting man, and a fine sportsman. It has always been so in England.

His old shipmates loved Lord Charles Beresford. I have seen old men of eighty—or ninety, or a hundred, for you cannot kill Queen Victoria's seamen—who had travelled miles to shake hands with their old officer, their seamed faces wrinkled with joy. " What, you remember me, Lord Charles? " And, " How could I ever forget you? " says the Admiral. In his *Memoirs*, Beresford prints a letter sent to him when he was writing that work, from an old topmate, a seaman in H.M.S. *Marlborough*, in which famous ship Beresford was a midshipman. " I think, my lord," writes Mr Lewis, fifty years after the event, " it would take me a little longer than thirteen seconds now to get to the main-topgallant yard-arm and run in again without holding on to anything, which I have done many hundreds of times." Wonderful old world of the Old Navy! Another old topmate, writing to Beresford in 1909, when the Admiral hauled down his flag and came on shore, says: "Going round Portsmouth dockyard some few years since, I was very sad to see the noble old *Marlborough*, a hulk, laid aside, as I expect we shall all be in time. I am doubtful if there are many men in the Navy to-day who would stand bolt upright upon the royal truck of a line-of-battle ship. I was one of those who did so. Perhaps a foolish practice. But in those days fear never came our way."

In that hard, noble, cheery school was Beresford nurtured, and fear never came his way from first to last. Those of later generations who would try to estimate Charles Beresford aright must learn somewhat of the Old Navy. The tall ships lie now in Port of Heaven. Their great seamen, Queen Victoria's admirals, are passing away, one by one, like the men of the old Victorian world on shore. Beresford was of the world of sailing line-of-battle ships, of Beaconsfield, of Gladstone, of Dickens, Thackeray, Tennyson, of Wolseley, and of Roberts. Beresford, almost alone among his contemporaries, held the secret of perpetual youth, taking each succeeding era as it came, wielding new forces with the same intuitive mastery, and preserving the same great-hearted magnanimity throughout all the shocks of fortune. " Now he belongs to the ages."

W. E. HENLEY

THE collected edition of the works of William Ernest Henley was published in 1908, in seven volumes, by David Nutt; and the right of publication was afterwards obtained by Messrs Macmillan, who, in publishing a collected edition, performed a notable service to English letters. The present writer is the fortunate possessor of the earlier editions : *London Voluntaries*, *The Song of the Sword*, *A Book of Verses*, *Views and Reviews*.

The influence of Henley has already extended beyond his own generation, and it will surely endure. Unfortunately, in his lifetime Henley made enemies. There is no need to discuss old controversies which should long since have been composed; it is enough to say that, like most differences, they originated in a misunderstanding which, it is ill to see, continues to inspire certain critics whose foible is jealousy. The lover of letters will do well to turn to the works themselves. In his little biography of *William Ernest Henley*, published by Messrs Constable, the present writer has tried to limn the man as he was.

William Ernest Henley was born in 1849. His influence was of that rare kind in which the personality is as potent as the written word. Nearly every writer of note among the young men of that epoch found in Henley wise counsel and generous encouragement, and drew inspiration from that magnificent and indomitable loyalty to the true and the beautiful which distinguished the master of his art. For Henley's conceptions of life and letters were his own; they had the force of nature.

Henley was before all a poet. He was also a critic in the sense of an interpreter. He could and did assail with a formidable onslaught the unworthy, the pretentious, and the base. But his criticism was the criticism of the seer. It is never true that a man is competent rightly to estimate that which he cannot in some measure do himself. Or, as one of the greatest among living critics has said, "he must have some knowledge of the process."

The little essays in *Views and Reviews* are models of interpretative criticism. They reveal, not defects which the reader can mark for himself but, beauties which only the interpreter who is also a poet can perceive and delineate; and which, being delineated, become a new possession. It is commonly argued by the younger generation that, as masterpieces can convey their own messages —or why masterpieces?—so the critic is a superfluous intermeddler. It is an ingenious theory, which has but one defect; it does not accord with the facts. That the critic is sometimes a superfluity, is nothing to the point, for in that case he is not an interpreter but something else : all sorts of respectable things, but not a critic.

Let us take as an example a passage from Henley's little appreciation of Herrick, which is only two pages long:

" In Herrick the air is fragrant with new-mown hay; there is a morning light upon all things; long shadows streak the grass, and on the eglantine swinging in the hedge the dew lies white and brilliant. . . . As you walk you are conscious of 'the grace that morning meadows wear,' and mayhap you meet Amaryllis going home to the farm with an apronful of flowers."

Or this passage from the essay on Longfellow:

" But Longfellow is the spokesman of a confraternity; what thrills him to utterance is the spirit of that strange and beautiful freemasonry established as long ago as when the first sailor steered the first keel out into the unknown, irresistible water-world, and so established the foundation of the eternal brotherhood of man with ocean."

It is true. The kindly American poet wrote of many things with charm and pleasant feeling, but when he writes of the sea his verse is suddenly informed with magic. But who save Henley saw it so clearly? And when he sees it, we see it also. And we also remember the noble prose in which the vision is limned. Henley dealt at close quarters with life as well as with literature; and hence it is that his influence inspired, besides men of letters, men of every rank and station and of most diverse characters.

Of his verse Henley gave to the world none

save his best, and his best ranks with the best in
English literature. The assertion can be no more
than an expression of an individual opinion. A
work becomes a classic by the slow accretion of
the individual opinions of those whose judgment
has authority; or, as Signor Benedetto Croce
affirms, by the accumulated judgment of mankind.
Not many of the contemporaries of Keats perceived
his true qualities; and we know where he immov-
ably stands to-day. There was no form in verse in
which Henley did not experiment; none in which
he did not turn the old form to new and often
magical purpose. He used ballade, rondeau,
villanelle and the rest. Here is an instance of
the traditional French form employed to a modern
and a vivid effect:

> The curtain falls, the play is played:
>   The Beggar packs beside the Beau;
> The Monarch troops, and troops the Maid;
>   The Thunder huddles with the Snow.
>   Where are the revellers high and low?
> The clashing swords? The lover's call?
>   The dancers gleaming row on row?
> Into the night go one and all.

And here, in the simplest metre, is irresistible
music:

> The nightingale has a lyre of gold,
>   The lark's is a clarion call,
> And the blackbird plays but a boxwood flute,
>   But I love him best of all.

Of his technical accomplishment, Henley perhaps sets most store by his unrhymed rhymes, a

form in which he accomplished a greater perfection than any poet has achieved before or since. Take the noble harmonies of the *London Voluntaries*, which open thus:

> St Margaret's bells,
> Quiring their innocent, old-world canticles,
> Sing in the storied air
> All rosy-and-golden, as with memories
> Of woods at evensong, and sands and seas
> Disconsolate for that the night is nigh.

The measure of the appreciation of a poet is the measure of the education and intelligence of the public. Hence, in Western civilization, there are few, compared with the mass of the people, who love poetry; and a new poet, ere he is known even to the few, must collect his readers, one here and another there, from among the multitude. It is the hope of democracy that one day all shall be enlightened. During his lifetime, sad to say, Henley was little known even in his own country, and less in America; though he needed the money which reputation brings. The wealth of his bequest to all who speak the English tongue, which I have tried to indicate, each must appropriate for himself.

A GROUP OF AUTHORESSES

WITH the death in 1921 of Lady Gilbert, who wrote her strange fantastic Irish romances under her maiden name of Rosa Mulholland, the last of a group of Victorian women writers has gone from us. Miss Thackeray (afterwards Lady Ritchie), Miss Yonge, Mrs Walford, Mrs Ewing, and the delightful American authoress, Louisa M. Alcott: all have departed, but their books remain, a notable estate in the heritage of English letters. Of another kind were George Eliot, Mrs Oliphant, Mrs Gaskell, Mrs Henry Wood, Miss Braddon, Rhoda Broughton, and the magnificent Ouida—to name but these. For these gifted ladies wrote not for young people—for whom, indeed, their books were considered not proper—but for the great world. The group among whom one might venture to assign primacy to Miss Thackeray, wrote for girls and young women, and they wrote exceedingly well. They were of a sweet and a high nature, loving the simple things which girls love; inspired with a perfect enthusiasm for honest friendship, the domestic affections, the home, the family, the schoolroom fire, and the flowers in the garden. These admirable women possessed a singular purity of spirit, so that they perceived, with the wonder and delight of the child, all things fresh and clean and as if new created, nor did the passage of the years dim their vision. Their books exhale an air of fragrant innocence : an innocence which is not ignorance of evil but the renunciation of evil. All were women schooled by sorrow and learned in cares, walking composedly in a harsh world, confident in faith.

They wrote to please the young people whom they loved, and with a thought, perhaps, to instruct as well as to entertain. Certainly Miss Yonge never failed to inculcate a moral, for indeed that estimable lady was a stern moralist, austerely High Church, and set about her business very seriously. But with all her piety she owned a gift of romance, and her work was touched with poetry. Who that read *The Dove in the Eagle's Nest* in youth can recall without a thrill those vivid and emotional adventures in that enchanted setting?

Mrs Ewing, alone among her contemporaries, possessed a particular appreciation of soldiers, and the ring and stir of arms. She knew something of that plain and noble character of the British soldier which Mr John Fortescue, the historian of the British Army, has limned with so fine an appreciation. Honest, cheery, grumbling, chivalrous, invincibly kind-hearted, profoundly humorous, the British soldier in his time has set his ammunition boot upon the neck of Europe; but whether beaten—but he has never remained beaten, and is in fact invincible—or victorious, he has ever won the affection of his antagonists. Mrs Ewing, to her honour, saw the Service Man as he superbly is; saw, too, the child's instant recognition of his worth; and so her brave and sorrowful little stories were read wherever all the world over British bugles sound at sunset and at dawn.

Mrs Walford treated of the home and the adventures of the hearth; sentimental, sensible, good-humoured stories, as jolly to-day as when they were written; but depicting a society very different from our own. In Queen Victoria's earlier reign the ideal of the English home attained its apotheosis. To the Queen herself, stateswoman as she was, her home was the supreme and sacred interest of her life, and her influence upon society was extraordinary. It is true, as Mr Lytton Strachey has remarked, that the English people loved the Queen because she was above all a home-maker, regarding her people rather as an extension of her household; but it is also true that the Queen's example impressed millions of good folk. Her Ministers made England powerful; the Queen made England good.

Louisa Alcott wrote of American households, but save for a few turns of speech and one or two variations in manners, there is nothing to distinguish the March family from an English family of the period. Forty years or so since, there was scarce an English home which did not treasure *Little Women* and *Good Wives*; and these perennially fascinating works are still read.

The charming works of Miss Thackeray are of another class. She grew up in the world of society, sharing her father's work and her father's friends.

Her style has much of Thackeray's wonderful ease and consummate mastery. He used often to dictate to her parts of the novel on which he was at work. In the Library of Trinity College, Cambridge, are manuscripts in which Miss Thackeray's hand appears upon many consecutive pages, clear and rather large. There are very few corrections, either in the dictated passages or in her father's precise small script. Miss Thackeray, bred as she was in the great world, and received everywhere, did not write of society, save in her delightful books of reminiscences, in which from first to last there is never an ungracious word nor an unkind reflection. She wrote tender and rather melancholy stories, bathed in a gentle atmosphere as of a spring evening, with a fragrance of lilacs in the air, and a wistful calling of birds as the sun goes down in a clear sky.

Miss Thackeray, in despite of delicate health and of many difficulties, was always writing, and always made a small annual income from her works. In her middle age she married Richmond (afterwards Sir Richmond) Ritchie, whom she survived. Lady Ritchie, and Lady Ritchie alone, could have written the life of William Makepeace Thackeray, had he not forbidden the task. To the "Gold Pen" collected edition of her father's works, Lady Ritchie contributed prefaces, written with a tantalizing tact and an admirable skill, which deftly indicate in what circumstances each book was written. In her volume of essays, her subtle sketches of the notable persons whom she knew—

and she knew all notable persons—are masterpieces of their kind.

Children and young people had no more generous and loving friend than Anne Thackeray Ritchie. In her books she gave them of her best. Her innumerable deeds of kindness are enshrined in many memories. She was never rich, for her books were too finely wrought to be popular, yet she was perpetually giving. Had she been rich, she would have still given away all except what would barely have sufficed her frugal needs. She loved giving, and her gifts were bestowed with an incomparable grace, so that every kindness was a work of art, whose fashion had its own inestimable value.

Lady Ritchie possessed all her father's immense beneficence of heart. Thackeray would—and did —risk his whole fortune to save a friend, and toiled his life long to leave his children the same modest patrimony with which himself had been endowed; which he had lost, and which he regained. And it was his passionate hatred of cruelty and his steady scorn of shams which made him to deal vengefully with all sorts of painted imposture. Not so his daughter. Lady Ritchie, gifted with all her father's shrewd perception and indomitable sincerity, retained throughout all vicissitudes an unfaltering sweetness of temper and a serene devotion to beautiful things. Lady Ritchie saw the splendour and the squalor, so strangely mingled, of the great Queen's reign; she knew the England of Dickens and Tennyson and Browning, of William Morris and Rossetti and Millais; she recalled the smiling country-side scarce marred by railways, and London at a time when she walked through green fields from Kensington to Earl's Court; and dwelt in France and Germany and Italy at a time when even poor people could travel and live there happily. She beheld the world change and darken, and endured the calamity of the Great War, of which she did not live to see the end. . . . Anne Thackeray Ritchie lives now in the memories of those who knew her, most notable and gracious among Victorian women; and her books, charming like a grave melody played in tune, tell of honour and love and courage, of gay and gentle people, and of the good which is found in all men and women.

LADY BANCROFT

ᢞ

LADY BANCROFT, born Marie Effie Wilton, was one of the most charming and gifted actresses of the mid-nineteenth century, when the tradition of English comedy with all its robust and innocent merriment was restored to the stage. Marie Wilton herself became a leader in the revival of the school of Sheridan and Goldsmith, when, in 1865, with splendid pluck, the penniless little actress started management on her own account, with a thousand pounds lent to her by her brother-in-law, Mr Francis Drake. Marie Wilton took the Queen's Theatre in Tottenham Street, a small and a neglected house, commonly called the Dust Hole, and engaged the exclusive services of H. J. Byron to supply her with plays of the burlesque type, of which that playwright was a master. The theatre, renamed the Prince of Wales's, was painted and cleaned and furnished; Marie Wilton played in a Byronic burlesque or two; and thenceforward her fortune was assured.

It was at this time Marie Wilton came to the rescue of a young playwright, Tom Robertson, whose comedy, *Society*, had been refused by every prominent manager in London. Robertson was suffering the usual consequences of attempting something new in dramatic art. Rejecting the artificial and outworn convention of the day, the absurd melodrama played in the ridiculous manner (which still survives) of false emphasis and unreal declamation, Robertson drew life as he saw it. That Marie Wilton, trained, as she had been trained, in the artificial modes of the theatre since she was a small child, should have perceived the merit of Robertson's work, is a singular testimony to her judgment. In accepting the new play at a moment when her whole future depended upon her success, she manifested a notable courage. Her judgment and her courage were alike justified. *Society*, produced in November 1865, Marie Wilton playing Maud Hetherington and Mr Bancroft playing Sidney Daryl, ran for one hundred and fifty nights, a very long run in those days.

The production of Robertson's *Society* marked the revival of true English comedy, in which life was truthfully delineated and truthfully presented. There followed a series of the jolly Robertson pieces : *Ours*, *Caste*, *Play*, *School*, and *M.P.* In 1867, Marie Wilton married Squire Bancroft; and in 1879, Mr and Mrs Bancroft took the Haymarket Theatre. Mrs Bancroft describes her grief at leaving the Prince of Wales's, in which so many delightful years of hard work had passed. As she went from room to room bidding them farewell, the very walls, she said, seemed to reproach her.

At the Haymarket the Bancrofts happily continued their successful management. They retired in 1885, with a fortune won by twenty years of hard work in which they honestly gave the public of their best. Among the plays they produced, and in which they acted, besides the Robertson comedies, were: W. S. Gilbert's *Sweethearts*; Wilkie Collins's *Man and Wife*; Reade and Taylor's *Masks and Faces*, which is the dramatized version of Charles Reade's admirable novel, *Peg Woffington*, the heroine being played to perfection by Mrs Bancroft; *The School for Scandal*, *The Vicarage*, *Money*, *Diplomacy*, *Fédora*, and *Lords and Commons*. Never, perhaps, has any management given a like entirely delightful and an invariably refined entertainment; and the name of the Bancrofts will long be honoured.

Lady Bancroft began to learn her art almost as soon as she could walk and talk. One among a large and a needy family, she helped to earn money by reciting and playing infantine parts. She relates how she was sometimes roused from bed late at night, carried to the theatre, and led upon the stage, when she was still so sleepy, poor little girl, that she began to recite the wrong piece.

As a child, she played at the theatres of Bath and Norwich, and was a member of the company at Bristol under J. H. Chute. In the same theatre were trained Ellen Terry, Mrs Kendal, Henrietta Hodson, and Charles Coghlan. Little Marie Wilton played Fleance in one of Macready's farewell performances of *Macbeth*, and after the play the great actor sent for the child. She told him her ambition was to play Lady Macbeth.

"Oh," said Macready, "is that all! Well, I

like your ambition ; you are a strange little thing, and have such curious eyes ; but you must change them before you play Lady Macbeth, or you will make your audiences laugh instead of cry."

And, indeed, the girl made her audiences laugh instead of cry, and she had no need to regret her curious eyes, and that enchanting smile which endeared her to so many thousands.

In 1856, Marie Wilton was invited to play at the Lyceum in London. Although, as she recounts, it was with great trepidation that she accepted the proposal, she played the boy with great success in *Belphegor*; and then she played in William Brough's burlesque, *A Winter's Tale*. Thenceforward, for the next nine years, Marie Wilton played in burlesque at the Haymarket, at the old Adelphi, and at the Strand. She played the part then known as the ' burlesque boy' in these jovial pieces.

Dickens, who knew what he was talking about, having dropped into the Strand one night to see H. J. Byron's *The Maid and the Magpie*, wrote to Forster, " I call her the cleverest girl I have ever seen on the stage in my time, and the most singularly original." Her last appearance in burlesque was in Byron's *Little Don Giovanni*, in 1865. But all the time she aspired to play comedy, and this resolute woman fulfilled her ambition. She knew what she wanted and got it. To Lady Bancroft it was given, not only to succeed, but to exert a noble and an enduring influence upon the art she loved.

A writer in *The Times*, who remembered her playing, upon the death of Lady Bancroft in 1921 recorded that "playgoers have long grown used to doing without her acting. The roguish eye, the infectious laughter, the delicious little moves, and the mingled archness, sweetness, petulance, grace and sauciness—let us add the compelling dignity and beautiful movements of the little figure —have long disappeared from the stage. Few actresses, perhaps, have roused such warm feelings of personal devotion in the public as Lady Bancroft. Her farewell appearance at the Haymarket, and her reappearance in *Diplomacy*, were scenes of indescribable enthusiasm. The constant unselfishness with which she subordinated herself to the demands of the *ensemble*, playing a small part or even no part at all when the occasion demanded it, deserves honourable recognition. In the theatre, as in private life, her ready sympathy, her quick but kindly wit, and her irresistible charm endeared her to all with whom she came in contact."

A veteran actor, who was a member of the Bancrofts' company, told the present writer that the Bancrofts' management was the first to treat actors and actresses with courtesy and consideration. Instead of lining up in a queue, for instance, to receive their pay, the members of the company received their salaries with that decorous privacy proper to ladies and gentlemen. It may seem a small matter, but it was significant of much.

To have made so many honest people happy; to be remembered by them with respect and affection ; to have achieved a consummate skill in a chosen art ; and to have raised the standard of that art, establishing a fresh and a clean tradition of innocent mirth ; how good and pleasant the life of little Marie Wilton and Lady Bancroft.

By way of excursion into the obvious, it is commonly said that the player, unlike other artists, leaves no memorial of his achievement for the benefit of posterity. No more does the executant musician, the schoolmaster, the clergyman — the bishop even. And it may be suggested that the loss to posterity causes them no anxiety. As for the people who are not artists, some millions die every year whose work is also unknown to posterity, yet their survivors are not discouraged. It is a melancholy reflection, nevertheless, that good work should perish in oblivion. The truth is, it does not so perish. There is of course another favourite excursion into the obvious, to the effect that the departed and their completed task live in the memories of those who remain. Yet these too must pass ; so that the platitudes of moralists who are afraid to believe in a future life appear singularly unconsoling. It is, however, not an article of faith but a fact that nothing is wasted, nothing lost ; and those who delighted in the art of Marie Bancroft need not waste regret upon the fall of the curtain at the interval.

II : *PERSONS* (2)

DANTE

THE extant memorials of the life of Dante
Alighieri are like a series of frescoes adorn-
ing the sun-shadowed wall of an Italian
cloister, dimmed by time, partly effaced, with
here and there a salient and a vivid image.
Here is limned a majestic figure, his brows
encircled with a laurel wreath, walking amid
the luminous Italian landscape of rounded hills
and fair valleys; here a distant castle poised
upon a crag, there a gay troop of horsemen
winding far away; or seated in his chamber,
bent upon a great book; or standing aside from
the clash of a tournament, wholly immersed in
the volume in his hand; or fighting in the fore-
front of the battle between Guelf and Ghibelline,
joined upon the plain of Campaldino; or seated
in the Prior's chair, guiding the ruling council
of his native Florence; and then, a solitary
figure, riding slowly towards the towered city
set among the vineyards, seeking an exile's
shelter.

In truth, as little is known of Dante as of
Shakespeare. The historians busy themselves
with the discussion of conjectures, refusing to
accept records the evidence for which they
cannot verify. The life of Dante, written by

Ser Boccaccio, who was eight years old at the close of Dante's life, is both the despair of the conscientious historian and the delight of its readers; for of writing history, as that operation is understood to-day, the cheerful artist Boccaccio recked little. He was wholly concerned to paint a beautiful picture, embellishing it with his delightful eloquence. Leonardo Bruni Aretino wrote a brief biography of Dante, which, except in one particular, is regarded by the critics as accurate so far as it goes. The two Villanis, Giovanni and his nephew, Filippo, also wrote short lives of the poet. These chroniclers set down what they knew, which was little, and also what they thought, which was much.

Dante was born in the city of Florence in the year 1265. He passed into the other land, which he knew already in a vision, from the city of Ravenna in 1321. In the time into which he was born, a man's allegiance was claimed by his own city. The idea of government, outside the self-governing city, was a theocracy of the world, of which His Holiness the Pope was Vicar on earth, and the Emperor of the Holy Roman Empire the Pope's vicegerent. In practice, the Papacy and the Empire were rivals for supremacy; and, broadly speaking, of the two parties which were ever at war with each other, the Guelfs were for the Church and the Ghibellines were for the Empire; and these two main divisions were

subdivided into various raging factions, such
as the Bianchi and the Neri: of all which
quarrels let the distracted history of the period
discourse.

Among those confused and passionate dis-
putes moved Dante, following his star. Sprung
of an ancient and a respectable, though not
an ennobled, family, Dante inherited the tradition of civic duty; as a young man he was a
friend of the learned statesman Brunetti Latini,
and, it seems, of the young King of Hungary,
Carlo Martello; and he steadfastly bore his
part in the conduct of affairs as a gentleman
should.

From his boyhood upwards Dante seemed to
have studied intensely. He " gave up his whole
boyhood," writes Boccaccio, " in his own city, to
unbroken study of the liberal arts, and became
wondrous expert therein. . . . And perceiving
that the works of the poets are not vain and silly
fables or marvels, as many witless ones suppose,
but have concealed in them the sweetest fruits of
historical or philosophical truth, so that the full
conceptions of the poets may not be wholly had
without history and moral and natural philosophy,
thereupon duly dividing out his time, he strove to
master history by himself, and philosophy under
divers teachers, not without long study and toil.
. . . In his youth he took the greatest delight
in music and song; and with all the best singers
and musicians of those times he was in friendship
and familiarity; and many a poem was he drawn

on by this delight to compose. . . ." Thus
Boccaccio.

Leonardo Bruni adds, " But for all this he did
not shut himself up at ease, nor sever himself from
the world, but living and moving about among
other young men of his age, he approved himself
gracious and skilful and valiant in every youthful
exercise; in so much that in that memorable and
most mighty battle that was fought at Campaldino, he, being of military age and well seen
to, found himself under arms, fighting strenu-
ously, mounted among the fore-fighters. . . .
When Dante returned from this battle he gave
himself up to his studies more fervently than
ever, but nevertheless maintained all his social
and civic intercourse. And it was wonderful
how, though he studied without cessation, no
one would have supposed from his gay style
and youthful company that he was studying
at all." [1]

Thus Dante lived, not indeed a double life, but
a life in the world whose conduct was illumined
by a secret flame. And of that inward fire let
Boccaccio, in his own delightful way, relate the
kindling. " In that season wherein the sweetness
of heaven reclothes the earth with its adornments,
making her all to smile with diversity of flowers
mingled amongst green leaves, it was the custom
both of men and women in our city, each in his
district, to hold festival, gathering together in

---

[1] The quotations are taken from the excellent translation by
Philip H. Wicksteed of *The Early Lives of Dante*.

their several companies; wherefore it chanced
that Folco Portinari, amongst the rest, a man
in those days much honoured of the citizens,
had gathered his neighbours round about, to
feast them in his house on the first day of
May.

"Now amongst them was that little Alighieri
already spoken of; and thither (even as little
lads are wont to go about with their fathers,
especially to places of festivity) Dante, whose
ninth year was not yet ended, had accompanied
him.

"And here, mingling with the others of his
age—for in the festal houses were many of them,
boys and girls—the first tables being served, he
abandoned himself with the rest to children's
sports, so far as the compass of his small years
would extend. There was amongst the throng of
young ones a little daughter of the aforesaid Folco,
whose name was Bice (though he himself always
called her by the original of the name, to wit,
Beatrice), whose age was some eight years; right
gracious after her childish fashion, and full gentle
and winning in her ways, and of manners and
speech far more sedate and modest than her small
age required; and besides this the features of her
face full delicate, most excellently disposed, and
replete not only with beauty but with such purity
and winsomeness, that she was held of many to
be a kind of little angel. She then, such as I
am painting her, or maybe far more beauteous
yet, appeared before the eyes of our Dante, at this

festival, not I suppose for the first time, but for the first time with power to enamour him; and he, child as he still was, received her fair visage into his heart with such affection, that, from that day forth, never, so long as he lived, was he severed therefrom. . . ."

According to Dr Butler, " It is from Boccaccio, and from him alone, that we have learned to see in Dante's mystical guide and guardian, in the lost love of his early years, only the idealized and allegorized figure of Folco Portinari's daughter." And Dr Butler adduces evidence supporting Boccaccio's story. Dante followed the chivalric idea of his time, which ordained that a man should love one woman supremely, above and beyond all other earthly ties; so much we know, and that is all. It is said that Beatrice Portinari married Simone de Bardi; and that Dante's friends persuaded him to marry Mistress Gemma, of the family of the Donati, probably about the year 1294.

Of his life at this period Leonardo Bruni writes : " He had a very good house in Florence, next to that of Geri di Messer Betto, his associate; possessions in Camerata, in the Placentina and in Piano di Ripoli; and abundant and choice furniture, as he says. He was a man of remarkably polished manners, of reasonable height, and of pleasant aspect, full of gravity; a slow and infrequent talker, but very keen in retort. . . . His chief pursuit was poetry, not of the barren, poor and fantastic sort, but impregnated and enriched and confirmed by true knowledge and many disciplines."

At this time, towards the end of the thirteenth century, Dante took part in the conduct of public affairs. The government of the city of Florence was then vested in a committee of six Priors, who held office for two months. A Prior must be a member of a Guild. The trading Guilds were called Arts. There were seven Greater and five Lesser Arts. Dante belonged to the *Speziali*, or dealers in spices, one of the Greater Arts, which perhaps included booksellers.

In 1300, Dante was chosen as one of the Priors, and at once became involved in the troubles of the time. The two factions of the Bianchi and the Neri had come to blows, thus dividing the Guelfs against themselves. The leaders of the Guelfs, in order to prevent the Ghibellines from taking advantage of the situation, asked the Pope to act as mediator between Blacks and Whites. Pope Boniface VIII (Benedetto Guatani) sent the Cardinal of Ostia, Matthew of Acquasparta, to perform that office. His advice was declined, and after promulgating—as a matter of form— an edict, the Cardinal returned to Rome. The Neri then resolved to ask the Pope to summon aid from France; whereupon the Priors arrested the Neri leaders, some of whom were banished. But, in 1301, Charles of Valois, brother of the King of France, entered Florence, ostensibly to make peace; actually, to bring civil war into the city. In 1302, the White Party were driven from Florence, and with them Dante, who had steadily resisted all external interference with the government of the city. He never again beheld Florence.

Thenceforward was Dante an exile; and thenceforward his work was the composition of the great poems. He dwelt at Verona; at Lucca; perhaps he visited Paris and Bologna; finally he went to Ravenna.

It is recorded by Boccaccio that, when Dante dwelt in his first city of refuge, Verona, " as he passed by a gateway where sat a group of women, one of them said to the others, softly, yet so that she was heard well enough by him and by his company : ' Do you see the man who goes to hell, and comes again, at his pleasure; and brings tidings up here of them that be below? ' To the which one of the others answered in all good faith : ' In truth it must needs be as thou sayest. See'st thou not how his beard is crisped and his skin darkened by the heat and smoke that are below? ' And hearing these words spoken behind him and perceiving that they sprang from the perfect belief of the women, he was pleased, and as though content that they should be of such opinion, he passed on smiling a little."

Beside that picture we may set another, limned by one " Brother Ilario, a humble monk of Corvo," who relates how Dante came one day to Ilario's monastery. " And when I saw him (as yet unknown to me, and to the rest, my brothers) I asked

him what he sought ; and when he answered never
a word, and yet kept on gazing at the architecture
of the place, I asked him again what he sought.
Then he, looking round upon me and the brothers,
said, ' Peace.' "

MOLIÈRE

WHO was this Molière, this French playwright and artist of the seventeenth century, whose works are read and performed to-day, when whole generations of plays between his time and ours have perished utterly? Jean-Baptiste Poquelin, called Molière, the son of Jean Poquelin, upholsterer to the King, was born in 1622 and died in 1673, in which year his last play was produced. There is no better introduction to the study of Molière than Mr Arthur Tilley's *Molière* (published by the Cambridge University Press); and the best way of using it is to read, first, the brief biography; then to turn to the plays, reading each play before reading Mr Tilley's commentary upon it.

In his mastery of the art of the theatre, Molière ranks with Shakespeare. The two great artists were singularly unlike each other; but they were alike in this, that in the work of both an old tradition ended and a new epoch in art began. They were alike, too, in that both were masters of their craft, perfected by continuous hard work.

Molière was at once actor and playwright almost from the beginning. After 1645, Molière and his troupe of players, having made a failure in Paris, wandered for thirteen years in the provinces. It is known that Molière's *Le Dépit amoureux* was performed in 1656, and that his first regular play, *L'Étourdi*, was performed in the same or in the preceding year. Molière returned to Paris in 1658, when the young Louis XIV was seventeen years of age. Thenceforward the King was the patron and the protector of the fearless playwright, who delighted to hold up to ridicule the follies of the age, and who dared even to satirize the fashions of the Court itself.

Much has been written concerning Molière's style, Molière's construction, Molière's habit of "taking his goods where he found them," Molière's moral teaching, and the like. Not so much, perhaps, concerning Molière's supreme and shining virtue, which consisted in his invincible determination to make his theatre entertaining, amid a world compounded of tedious pedantry and dubious farce. First and last, Molière sought to amuse; and his method was high comedy. Like all great artists, he set himself to achieve his enterprise within certain strict limitations. He would not offend morality nor infringe the rules of good taste. French manners are not our manners; morals and conventions change; and if there be aught in Molière's pages which we dislike, we may be assured that he did not transgress the code of his times.

In the practice of his art Molière passed from the artificial to reality. The stage at that period was peopled by accepted and familiar types: the valet, the chambermaid, the husband, the wife, the father, the pair of lovers. These were all stock characters. The playwright exhibited one characteristic in each person, and in each person it was always the same. In England, there was the same tradition, which Shakespeare reformed and renewed, and which was known as the representation of what were called Humours. Persons were not represented, save in one aspect; and in the result, the convention became farther and farther removed from life, and at the same time dull. The public, weary of the classic French playwrights with their interminable Alexandrines and their faded imitation of the antique, and bored by the common farces of the Hôtel Bourgogne, did not know what they wanted. But Molière knew, and he gave it to them. He gave of his best. His business was to amuse; he provided the best possible amusement, designed by a singularly intelligent man for rational people; and he had his reward.

In order to delineate people, said Molière, you must paint from nature. He disdained the ruling artifice, and presented real persons on the stage. They still exhibited, as all characters represented on the stage must exhibit, one salient aspect of their personality; but the rest of that personality is indicated as well. Molière drew not from the flat but from the round. It does not follow that he transplanted to the boards actual characters from life, though it is said that he occasionally deliberately copied a particular person. Molière's method was to study character by means of assiduous observation, and to represent its essence on the stage. It is for this reason (among others) that his persons are alive to-day; and that the ridicule of a transient fashion as, for instance, in *Les Précieuses ridicules*, is still amusing, although the fashion itself has long passed away.

Molière is the supreme exponent of the art of pure comedy. As it was his business to amuse good people—*les honnêtes gens*—in the best way, so he wrote comedy; and, himself an incomparable actor, he played comedy. Behind his noble bequest of honest and innocent laughter stands the man himself, the indomitable worker, the skilled craftsman, kindly, sensitive, humorous, and, above all, humane: Molière the good.

The plays of Molière are taught in schools as exercises in the French language; with the usual result, that the pupil regards the French author as writing for the instruction of the fifth form; much as he, or she, regards Julius Cæsar as composing a history of his dreary wars in Gaul for the edification of the elementary Latin class. It is a mistake. Molière—it is really necessary to remark —wrote for the stage; and there is but one way to appreciate his work, which is to witness its performance by the admirable players of the first theatre in Europe, the Comédie Française. Every gesture, every intonation and movement, of these accomplished actors is studied in the detailed records which are kept in the theatre, and in which are described exactly how each great actor in his turn interpreted the classic parts. There is no such tradition in England, nor can Englishmen rightly interpret the classic French comedy. The French play it with extreme rapidity and perfect finish. It is partly by reason of their swift elocution that they can hold their audiences during the long speeches with which the French playwrights inspire their characters.

If the plays of Molière, then, cannot for lack of opportunity be witnessed, and must be read, let them be studied with the picture of the bright, neat French stage ever in the mind, together with the imagined gesture, movement, and expression of the actors; and, above all, with the idea of speed in action and in elocution.

Molière, as a young man, began by writing farces, or rewriting existing farces, which were a development of the tradition of mediæval farce, defined by M. Gaston Paris as " the representation in verse of a scene in private life; it is short and has few characters; it generally introduces us to the interior of a lower-class household. . . ."

Playing for some time at Lyons, in which town Italian taste predominated, Molière refashioned some old Italian farces and comedies. Two of these are included in his published works: *Le Médecin volant* and *La Jalousie du Barbouillé*. Molière's first regular comedy, *L'Étourdi*, was founded upon the Italian comedy *L'Inavvertito*, by Nicolò Barbieri. The theme is simply the continual defeat of the ingenious stratagems of Mascarille, the cunning valet, by the stupidity of his master, Lélie. It is conventional Italian comedy throughout, distinguished by Molière's admirable verse. His next play was also taken from an Italian piece, Nicolò Secchi's *L'Interesse*, to which Molière added much of his own.

In *Les Précieuses ridicules*, produced in Paris in 1659, Molière achieved his first original play in the purely French manner. In this piece, the characters, instead of being named with conventional titles, as in the Italian manner, are called after the actors who played the parts, according to the French fashion. Thus there are Grange and Du Croisy, the two lovers, and the two *Précieuses* are named respectively Madelon, after Madeleine Béjart, and Cathos, after Catherine de Brie. Marotte, the servant's name, was the theatrical name of Marie Ragueneau. Almanzor, the lackey, was thus named by the *Précieuses* of the play after a character in one of the long heroic romances of the day, Gomberville's *Alexandre*. Gorgibus is a name taken from life. Mascarille, as the conventional name of a valet, is retained.

In *Les Précieuses ridicules*, Molière adventured into what was then the almost unexplored region of social satire, of which he became the sovereign exponent. He went on to produce *Les Fâcheux*, *L'École des Maris*, and *L'École des Femmes*. Then came *Tartuffe*, of which piece the Church profoundly disapproved. Its performance was prohibited, and Molière produced *Don Juan*, his version of the legend which was first dramatized by Tirso de Molina, the Spaniard, about 1630.

There followed *Le Misanthrope*, *Amphitryon*,

a mythological piece, *George Dandin*, *L'Avare*, various comedy-ballet plays, and *Le Bourgeois Gentilhomme*, which was a *comédie-ballet*.

In that excellent play Molière improved upon the old French tradition of the ballet, which "consisted," says Mr Tilley, "of *Récits*, *Entrées*, and *Vers*." The recitations, which described the theme of the *Entrées*, or dances, were apparently a development of the Greek chorus of antiquity. The *Vers*, instead of being sung or said, were written or printed in the *livre de ballet* which was distributed among the spectators, and served as a kind of explanatory chorus. Molière welded these separate elements into a coherent whole. The *comédie-ballet* has survived in various forms.

Molière returned to the social comedy proper in *Les Femmes savantes*, presented in 1672. His last piece, *Le Malade imaginaire*, a *comédie-ballet*, was produced in the following year. The playwright himself took the name-part, despite the far from imaginary illness with which he was stricken. He played to the last; he was dying as he played; and one night the curtain fell upon that gallant figure for the last time.

From first to last, Molière wrote to amuse. His gift was comedy, and he made the best of it. The supreme office of comedy is to hold up vice or folly to ridicule; and comedy must therefore proceed from a standard of morals; for in default of such a standard there could be no comparison drawn between what is and what ought to be, in which lively demonstration comedy consists. Molière's guiding star, said Faguet, is common sense. Mr Tilley observes that "common sense is the soul of comedy," and he adds that "if Molière's morality is modest and unambitious, it is at any rate sound and wholesome. . . . I have noted in connection with *Tartuffe* and *Don Juan* and *Le Misanthrope* how nearly Molière agrees with Bossuet and Bourdaloue. It is a striking testimony to the soundness of his morality that it should be possible to illustrate his attitude towards vice and wrong-doing from the sermons of the two great preachers who attacked his comedies with such uncompromising severity."

It may indeed be said that upon the quality of the great playwright's sense of morals depended his ability clearly to understand his material. Molière's perception of virtue was of a singular clarity, considerably exceeding the official standard of his time, and since. It is not always recognized that his indomitable determination to write in accordance with his ideal, defying the most powerful opposition and thereby risking his livelihood, proved at once Molière's invincible honesty and his indomitable courage. These qualities, indeed, are the mark of the artist; and to the artist of all time, Molière, like Shakespeare, remains the exemplar.

Dr Johnson, talking just a hundred years afterwards of Dr Goldsmith's new play, *She Stoops to Conquer*, said that "the great end of comedy" lay in "making an audience merry." For that extremely sensible remark the Doctor has been reproved by serious people. What would they have? It is a great gift to be able to amuse. It is among the greatest. And it is singularly rare. Goldsmith had it, and Sheridan; and these two artists, learning of Molière, did in their time for the English stage and the English people what Molière achieved for the French theatre and the French nation. They set out to amuse, and they did amuse. They set themselves to amuse within the rules of sound morality and good taste, and they succeeded. And if the serious persons think that is an easy business, let them try it. Let Heaven be witness, there needs no labour to be dull. The reader will remark it is even possible to write a dull essay upon Molière.

A QUEEN OF FRANCE

IN his admirable study of the Queen of France [1] the Marquis de Ségur, an historian of distinction, finds it incumbent upon him to disclaim any political bias. He finds no word of reproach for the men of the French Revolution. His detachment is perfect. He is solely concerned to relate what is in truth a tragedy according to the classic definition.

Marie Antoinette, the Austrian princess, from the moment of her marriage with the Dauphin, who became Louis XVI of France, entered all unknowing into a coil of circumstance which she did not understand, in which she became enmeshed beyond help, and from which she was only released by the guillotine. For the condition of France at the time of the little princess's entrance into France the student must consult the histories of the period, of which Carlyle's *French Revolution* remains the best; and the admirable studies of M. Le Nôtre contain the result of later researches. The Marquis de Ségur assumes a general knowledge of history on the part of his readers. His purpose is to paint the portrait of the Queen, and to indicate only those events of the time which serve to illustrate her character. Indeed, the historian vividly

[1] *Marie Antoinette*, by the Marquis de Ségur (Paris, Calmann-Lévy).

69

demonstrates how powerful is the influence of character upon events, as distinguished from the effect of deliberately planned political measures. The Queen, for instance, was judged by her French subjects rather for what she was—or, to be more precise, for what they thought she was —than for what she actually did; and again and again when they had condemned her unheard for a political policy, often falsely attributed to her influence, the fickle populace were charmed for the moment by her personal grace and kindliness of heart into forgiving her. What they never really pardoned was the Queen's extravagance, to which the people—wrongly, as usual—attributed the intolerable taxation imposed upon them.

Moreover, from the first, the French disliked the reign of a foreigner. Throughout, they distrusted *l'Autrichienne*. The marriage was of course arranged entirely in the interests of the reigning dynasties and for diplomatic reasons; and few alliances more poignantly illustrate the absolute subordination of the welfare of a whole nation to the dynastic convenience of its rulers. Doubtless the assumption was that the welfare of the people was best served by confirming the power of sovereignty among the royal houses of Europe, a purpose usually accomplished by means of intermarriage among them. Thus the fortunes of a nation were made to hinge upon the domestic affairs of its King and Queen. The French Revolution was a violent protest against that practice, which, however, persisted and still persists.

"In the year 1764," writes the Marquis de Ségur, "emerged the project—however vague—of the marriage of Marie Antoinette with the Dauphin of France, the heir to the throne of Louis XV. That the project was essentially political, I need hardly affirm. The necessity for an alliance which should serve as a check to the ambitions of Prussia, and to the jealousies of England, and a bar to the aggression of Russia, influenced the Courts of Versailles and of Vienna to seal their union with a family tie." Exactly. And the little Marie Antoinette was educated strictly in accordance with this design. When she was thirteen (in 1768), her studies were entrusted to a Frenchman, the sagacious and learned Abbé de Vermond. Her mother, the Empress, "took pains to transform her daughter into the French likeness." She had a French hair-dresser and a French dentist. Her preceptors "taught her the customs of Versailles and the details of etiquette, and gave her lessons in the history of the eminent persons of the Court of Louis XV."

Such was the dismal fate of princesses. And on May 16, 1770, Marie Antoinette was married to the Dauphin. The Princess was under fifteen, the Dauphin was under sixteen, years of age. It was not until three years later that they made their formal entrance into Paris, amid the applause of the multitude.

" To the people of France," writes the Marquis de Ségur, " still devoted to the ancient dynasty—to this people so attracted by beauty, grace, and youth, yet so accustomed during more than a century to queens whom they never saw, and to princesses of distant manners and unattractive mien—this fair Archduchess, radiant and smiling, came like the blossoming of spring. The dawn of a new time, the hope of a future which should obliterate the miseries of the past and of the present, were signified in the word which passed upon every lip, the magic word at which every eye shone and every countenance brightened : ' *La Dauphine !* ' "

Such was the welcome accorded by her people to Marie Antoinette. How could she divine what lay in the future, or understand the mutability of popular sentiment? Gay, kind-hearted, innocent, the little Dauphine submitted to the monotonous routine of the dull Court, to the tedious asperities of the King's elderly sisters, to the incessant scoldings and admonitions received from her mother the Empress, whose design it was to induce Marie Antoinette to serve the political interest of Austria. A perfect mistress of unscrupulous and cynical intrigue, the Empress was perpetually writing to her daughter. Fortunately, the Dauphine did not take these dangerous epistles too seriously.

When the Dauphin succeeded his father as Louis XVI, and the Dauphine became Queen of France, she proceeded, like other queens in the same circumstances, to take her own way. Mesdames the aunts of the young King were promptly given to understand that their acidulated advice was no longer desired, and they were invited to retire to their provincial castle. The Queen arranged the Court according to her tastes. As for the King, he was perfectly happy so long as he was allowed to do as he liked. He liked hunting and hard exercise. He liked making things in a blacksmith's forge. He might have been good blacksr ith. He could never make a good King. He did not want to be a King. Intellectu exertion he abhorred. He could not make a cision; "an inability," says the historian, " hich was the chief fault of Louis XVI, the cause of all his failures, the origin of all his misfortunes."

The Queen, suddenly exalted to the autocratic sway of the most frivolous and luxurious society in the world; delivered from strict tutelage to an almost absolute freedom; young, vigorous, and in love with life; flung herself wholly into the pursuit of pleasure. Gaming, dancing, festivals, the chase, and a lavish extravagance: these dissipations absorbed her days and nights.

What else was the child to do? The King her husband avoided her. Owing to some defect of temperament, Louis was abnormally shy. Forced into a marriage of convenience, several years elapsed ere he dared a real marriage. The young Queen, quick with energy, vivacious, witty, charming, desiring motherhood yet childless, must do something. She remained faithful to her lord, but she took her wealth where she found it.

"In the life of Marie Antoinette," observes the historian, "there was a relatively brief period of about three years, which determined her fate . . . it lasted from the year 1775 to the end of 1778. . . . It was a phase of dissipation, of pleasure beyond reason, of prodigality without limit. In a word, it was a period of folly, of which, however, the consequences were terrible."

It was, in fact, a reaction from intense boredom. There seems no reason to suppose that the Queen incurred any reproach, other than the reproach of frivolity and (above all) of the most prodigal expenditure.

The French people were not offended by the pursuit of pleasure; but when the royal finances were exhausted, and the taxes, already intolerable, were increased, they became dangerously angry. Marie Antoinette, insisting upon choosing one minister of finance after another, selected charlatans who did but succeed in turning financial embarrassment into financial ruin. The people attributed their woes to their Queen. It was said that she owned three hundred horses, whereas the old Queen had but one hundred and fifty; that, in consequence, the royal stable cost an additional 200,000 francs; that the decorations of the Trianon were a constant and an immense expense;

that the festivals at Versailles were exceedingly
costly; that sinecures and pensions amounted to
an annual sum of 240,000 livres, and so "Déjà
se dessine la légende de la Reine insatiable
et dévoratrice de l'État, la légende meurtrière
de ' Madame Déficit,' " remarks the historian,
ominously.

Thus Marie Antoinette came to represent in
her own person excesses which, in fact, had
long been practised by the society of which she
had become the head. She became entangled
in the incessant political intrigues of a Court
in which honest men were few, and which was
totally unable to perceive that an accumulation of
disorders had made catastrophe almost inevitable.
Amid insoluble perplexities and perpetual em-
barrassments, Marie Antoinette, when she had
outworn her pleasures, constantly endeavoured
to fulfil what she believed to be her duty. The
King, except in matters of foreign diplomacy,
in the conduct of which he owned a kind of
hereditary skill, let all go, tacitly and with a
smiling indolence devolving his duties upon the
Queen.

In the hour of revolution, upon Marie Antoinette fell the main responsibility of saving the
throne, if it were possible to save it. Among
the revolutionaries, Lafayette and Mirabeau were
her friends. But the Queen probably distrusted
them, nor would she stoop to the acceptance of
their aid. "The King," said Lafayette to the
Marquess de Bouillé, " is a worthy person, who

possesses neither character nor courage, and with whom I could do what I will, if it were not for the Queen, who defeats me. Although she often shows confidence in me, she will never accept my advice, which would ensure her winning popularity. She has the qualities which would gain the hearts of the Parisians, but her hereditary pride, and a haughty temper which she knows not how to disguise, constantly alienate the people from her." Marie Antoinette, indeed, was born a princess of the blood royal; she would be gracious to her people, but to bargain or to make terms with revolutionaries was to suffer an intolerable humiliation.

Nevertheless, in her extremity, the Queen forced herself to treat with Mirabeau. Had he lived longer the Tribune might have saved the Queen. Danton failed her. That strange creature, the revolutionary Antoine Barnave, and his friends Lameth and Duterte, tried to save her and could not. The chivalrous Count Fersen, the faithful servant of Marie Antoinette, again and again risked his life in the attempt to rescue the Queen, and in vain. Surely here is one of the strangest episodes in history: the imprisonment and long-drawn sufferings of the Queen, the slow closing in of the relentless forces of her enemies, the invariable defeat of her friends. Her husband executed; her son torn from her; condemned to captivity under the perpetual vigilance of rough and brutal gaolers; brought to a cruel trial, alone, and sentenced; bound and carried through the roaring streets; the courage of the Queen endured to the last. A strange and a mysterious story.

"The last period of her life," writes the Marquis de Ségur, " cannot be the subject of judgment; it must be contemplated in silence. In the face of facts so eloquent, words are useless. I would confess, however—and I would that the reader feels it also—that in thus drawing near to the last of the queens of France, the sympathy towards her I have always entertained, is profoundly intensified. I believe that all those who at any time will impartially study the history of Marie Antoinette will feel the same. Innocently gay in prosperity, brave in conflict, pathetic in suffering, her history appeals in its every aspect to the heart of France; her character is endowed with all those qualities which attract and charm and invite sympathy; and her name will enchant the generations to come, so long as there are smiles of indulgence for the imprudences of youth, a tender regard for grace and beauty, and tears for misfortune."

What is one to think of such a tragedy as this? Scan the sequence of events as you will, there emerges no one point of which you can say, Here it began ; or, Had the Queen acted thus and thus instead of otherwise, catastrophe might have been avoided. It seems the affair was so immense, the accumulation of evil so formidable, that the individual was helpless. It happens so ; for every deed and word must have its exact consequence, in this world and in the next. As in the wicked city of Paris the Queen paid for the sins of others, so in the place to which she went, her grace and virtue preceded her and she was healed of sorrow.

VICTOR HUGO

✍

VICTOR HUGO, the last of the great French Romantics of 1840, was born in 1802 and died in 1885. At fifteen he obtained an honourable mention from the French Academy, to which august institution he had submitted a poem in competition for the annual prize. Thenceforward Hugo was the embodiment of France, alike in his life and in his work. First and last he was a poet. His verses will endure so long as the French tongue endures. He was a politician, inasmuch as he was the passionate champion of a cause. He sublimated France—her wars, revolutions, and catastrophes—and himself, in poetry: in poems, plays, and romances; but always in poetry. There was but one France, and one Victor Hugo, whose motto was *Ego Hugo*. From the young Royalist, who, taught by his mother, hated Napoleon Buonaparte, to the greatest man of letters in France and the apostle of freedom, hunted through the streets in the *coup d'état* of 1851, and thence to his exile in Guernsey, Victor Hugo, undefeated and indomitable, came to his own again in the France of 1870: the France of the Republic, the France of Flaubert, of the Daudets, the Goncourts, Mallarmé, Leconte de Lisle. Thereafter, the old monarch's reign was over; there were new ideas in art, and new men, and new poetry; and although Hugo was still acclaimed as the Master, it was but a nominal allegiance.

For the English student, perhaps the best life of the great Frenchman is the study of Victor Hugo written by Madame Duclaux.[1] Madame Duclaux, writes Mr Basil Williams, is "English by birth and French by long association," and (it seems) she writes in English, so that the discomfort of a translation is avoided, and we have a book in English written as a Frenchwoman would have written it. Madame Duclaux has done her work admirably well, and with an excellent sense of proportion.

In England, literature is singularly unaffected by politics, for the Englishman, and particularly the English artist, is bored by politics and hates disturbances. In France, which in the matter of art and literature is Paris, it is remarkably otherwise; and in order to appreciate the works of Victor Hugo, it is necessary to be familiar with the political events of the time. Such as these are seldom interesting in retrospect: and Madame Duclaux recounts no more than the essential outline.

In 1808, Victor's father, Colonel Hugo, was fighting in the Peninsular War under his master, King Joseph Buonaparte. The children were brought by Madame Hugo to Paris. "As a woman of thirty she still loved air, space, and a

[1] London, Constable and Co., "Makers of the Nineteenth Century" series, edited by Basil Williams.

noble adventure. She was to find them all in a roomy old house with a garden on the southern side of the Seine. It was a portion of the ancient convent of the Feuillantines left untouched by the Revolution : Impasse des Feuillantines, No. 12— an isolated mansion in a deserted quarter of the left bank of the Seine. The garden had long since run wild ; it was full of trees and birds, with in one corner a ruined chapel, less a town garden than a park, deep and vast, shut in by high walls, almost a field in the middle, at the edges almost a wood." In that ruined chapel, Madame Hugo hid a pro-scribed Royalist, General Lahorie ; and the old soldier was Victor Hugo's first schoolmaster.

It is probable that here were impressed upon Victor his most abiding memories ; nor did he ever forget that his kind old friend, his god-father, the veteran of La Vendée, after having been promised immunity from arrest, was taken and shot. . . .

Here is another picture, the description of the poet in his old age, occupied with " the disposal of an immense accumulation of manuscript, to which he was constantly adding. In literature as in life the methodical poet's watchword had been : waste not, want not ; and despite the serried volumes of his published works, his portfolios were full to over-flowing. . . . He composed even in the intervals of his fitful slumbers. His bed was surrounded with a sort of low dais, on which were laid pencils and sheets of paper ready to be superscribed with any stanza, happy line, or brilliant image that might occur to the poet in the watches of the night. . . . At nearly eighty years of age he still spent his mornings in writing, his afternoons in reverie and exercise. . . . Victor Hugo died at one o'clock in the afternoon on Friday, May 22, 1885. He had written in his will: 'I believe in God. I refuse the service of all the Churches: I beg a prayer from every soul.'"

There are a few great artists whose life and work are one; who transmute their personal experiences, their adventures, sorrows, passions, misfortunes, into drama and novel and verse. Among these was Victor Hugo. He beheld the giant shadow of Ego Hugo projected across the ages. Himself was the actor in tragedy and romance. Profoundly sensitive, perhaps not a little vain, Hugo believed that what happened to Hugo was of a tremendous importance. Did he fall in love, he expected the sun to stand still in the heavens. Was he persecuted? Then all the powers of darkness were leagued against him. Did he sometimes quit the good Madame Hugo for the solace of other ladies, had not Hugo the prerogative of genius? When he dreamed great dreams and beheld magnificent visions, rapt into another realm every afternoon, sunk in his reverie, was he not inspired by whatsoever god in whom he believed? His wild and towering fantasy held little converse with reason's sober remonstrance.

Hugo dwelt habitually with what we now call the unconscious mind. His method of writing seems to have been exactly the method prescribed to-day by the French scientific psychologists who teach the use of suggestion. Hugo placed his conscious faculties in abeyance, passing at will into a condition of trance, in which he passively noted all that came to him. Then he awoke and wrote. It may be that in the state of reverie, which is akin to the state of trance, he had access to another world which we are now beginning dimly to apprehend.

Withal, Hugo was a great poet, and a great and a courageous lover of France. The sturdy old patriot carried a musket in the war of 1870. Doubt not but that his strong and passionate spirit fought alongside the living in the Great War.

THE MAKING OF SIR WALTER

LOCKHART, the biographer of Sir Walter Scott, records that, together with Sir Walter, he visited Thomas Scott, Sir Walter's aged uncle. "I . . . thought him," writes Lockhart, "about the most venerable figure I had ever set my eyes on—tall and erect, with long, flowing tresses of the most silvery whiteness, and stockings rolled up over his knees, after the fashion of three generations back. He sat reading his Bible, and did not, for a moment, perceive that anyone had entered his room, but on recognizing his nephew he rose, with cordial alacrity, kissing him on both cheeks, and exclaiming, 'God bless thee, Walter my man! Thou hast risen to be great, but thou wast always good.'"

There, in a sentence, is Sir Walter Scott. He is among the greatest English men of letters; indeed, the present writer holds him to be the greatest; but he was more, for his whole life is an example of plain, honest, cheerful goodness. Lockhart's masterpiece of biography is both the most useful work the aspirant in literature can study, and the presentment of a noble exemplar.

On August 15, 1771, Walter Scott was born in his father's house (since pulled down) in College Wynd, Edinburgh. He was of gentle lineage, a circumstance which, in his view, imposed upon him certain inexorable obligations, inasmuch as the honour of an ancient line had descended to his keeping. He was proud of his race. He was proud of Scotland, loving intensely all that was great and fair and good in her troubled history, profoundly enamoured of crag and river and forest, thronged city and lonely tower.

As a child, he was stricken with infantile paralysis; and in order to restore his health, he was put to lie out on the fells all day, wrapped in a sheepskin. The shepherd who took care of him said that Walter " soon kenned every sheep and lamb by headmark as well as any of them." It was his first lesson in farming, and Scott became quite naturally a skilled agriculturist, like his forbears.

Scott tells us he was idle at school; it was a profitable idleness; for out of school hours he read history, travels, voyages, poetry. He found some odd volumes of Shakespeare in his mother's dressing-room, and read them by the light of the fire, when he should have been in bed. He read Ossian, which pretentious work did not quite please him. He knew by heart a great part of Spenser. He read Tasso and Percy's *Reliques*. Scott records that at this period of his life awoke " that delightful feeling for the beauties of natural objects which has never since deserted me. . . . The romantic feelings which I have described as predominating . . . naturally rested upon and associated themselves with these grand features of the landscape around me; and the historical incidents, or the traditional legends connected with many of them gave to my admiration a sort of intense impression of reverence, which at times made my heart feel too big for its bosom. From this time the love of natural beauty, more especially when combined with ancient ruins, or remains of our fathers' piety or splendour, became with me an insatiable passion. . . ."

At college, as at school, Scott rather slurred his prescribed studies, while pursuing his own researches with indefatigable zeal. In his fragment of autobiography, Scott affirms that he recollected lost opportunities " with the deepest regret," and " that I would at this moment give half the reputation I have had the good fortune to acquire, if by so doing I could rest the remaining part upon a sound foundation of learning and science." It is the utterance of a noble modesty. No man can know everything; and Scott knew more of his own subjects than any other student before or after him.

The Edinburgh of those days was a riotous as well as a learned city. To quote Henley's description of the Edina of Burns, it was " a city of clubs and talk and good fellowship, a city of harlotry and high jinks, a city (above all) of drink." Compare Sir Walter's own discreet picture, limned in *Guy Mannering*, of Colonel Mannering's discovery of Mr Paulus Pleydell, the advocate, on a Saturday night. " Mannering looked around him and could hardly conceive how a gentleman of a liberal profession and good society should choose such a scene for social indulgence. . . ."

In the old Edinburgh, then, the lad Walter Scott took his pleasure and his work with the zest of a brave and an innocent heart. What was evil he passed by. All that was good—the humour, jollity, kindliness, piety, scholarship— he absorbed.

Walter Scott, the father of Sir Walter, was a Writer to the Signet; and his son determined to enter the law as a barrister, after a term of apprenticeship in his father's office. Scott studied " with great ardour and perseverance." Here, indeed, was the test of the lad's character. He had no great liking for the law, but he saw it to be his duty to master his chosen profession; and during those four years he renounced the pursuits upon which his heart was set. Let it be observed that he was none the worse poet for that severe training. The discipline of the law forged his character. Scott the poet, Scott the editor, Scott the novelist, applied to literature the method, the common sense, the industry he acquired in his legal studies. He said afterwards that he " determined that literature should be my staff, but not my crutch," and that no man should rely upon literature for his livelihood, but should rather wear it as a bright feather in his cap. Wise counsel indeed; and the more weighty because Scott made a fortune by his pen.

He made no great figure at the Bar, a good deal to his disappointment; but he obtained the offices

of sheriff and of principal clerk of session, a post
which obliged him to attend in court during half
the year, for four or six hours daily. His duty was
to record the decisions of the Bench, a task demanding considerable legal knowledge and ability.
His livelihood was therefore comfortably secured.
That security, which would have lulled most men
to indolence, Scott used as the fulcrum for his
lever.

It was now that he began to work before breakfast. " He rose by five o'clock, lit his own fire
when the season required one, and shaved and
dressed with great deliberation—for he was a
martinet as to all but the mere coxcombries of
the toilet, not abhorring effeminate dandyism itself
so cordially as the slightest approach to personal
slovenliness, or even those ' bed-gown and slipper
tricks,' as he called them, in which literary men
are so apt to indulge. He was seated at his desk
by six o'clock, all his papers arranged before him
in the most accurate order, and his books of reference marshalled around him on the floor, while
at least one favourite dog lay watching his eye,
just beyond the line of circumvallation. Thus,
by the time the family assembled for breakfast
between nine and ten, he had done enough (in
his own language) ' to break the neck of the day's
work.' "

Active of body as he was, Scott, during his legal
apprenticeship, had accustomed himself to continuous sedentary labour. He had, upon occasions,
written " upward of one hundred and twenty folio

pages with no interval either for food or rest."
He possessed the scholar's memory, the faculty
of remembering accurately everything he read,
heard, observed. " My memory of events," he
writes, "was like one of the large, old-fashioned
cannons of the Turks—very difficult to load well
and discharge, but making a powerful effect when
by chance any object did come within range of its
shot."

Scott made himself a lawyer by dint of sheer
hard application. How did he become man of
letters, poet, novelist? By what means did he
win that vast treasury of knowledge, upon which
he drew steadily, day after day, before breakfast?
First, he was always reading, and all that he read
he remembered. Then, he explored the country-
side, collecting legends and stories, making acquaintance with all sorts and conditions of men.
There was no man, he used to say, from whom he
could not learn something, even in a chance conversation. He studied the effects of landscape and
the beauty of time-worn buildings with a constant
ardour.

For some curious reason he could not learn to
draw, although he set his energy and intellect,
which failed him in no other enterprise, resolutely
to the task. A similar inability is observable in
the case of Thackeray, who, although he was
trained as a painter, could not express in his
drawings the effects he so admirably depicted in
words. It was, however, the association of the
scene, rather than its form and colour, which Scott

appreciated. His feeling may best be understood in his delight, recorded by his friend Irving, in the first stanza of Meckle's *Cumnor Hall*.

> The dews of summer night did fall;
>   The Moon, sweet regent of the sky,
> Silver'd the walls of Cumnor Hall,
>   And many an oak that grew thereby.

Scott himself refers to the verses in his preface to *Kenilworth*, which delightful romance they partly inspired : " The first stanza especially had a peculiar species of enchantment for the youthful ear of the author," he wrote. The charm of the lines is either felt, or it is not. If it be appreciated, then something of the character of Scott's genius will be apprehended too.

To the present generation, Scott is known as poet and novelist, and his considerable labours in the rich estate of English literature are partly forgotten. He did a great deal of excellent work in editing English classical authors. He wrote their biographies. He kept his friend, James Ballantyne the publisher, whose fortunes Scott founded, occupied in printing edition after edition of various works. Thus did Scott acquire the solid critical understanding of the great English tradition in literature, which he so nobly maintained and so prodigally enriched.

In France, the work of Scott, by a singular inversion of the fact, was regarded as romantic, as distinguished, in the French sense, from the classical. In truth, Scott was an exponent of the

English classical tradition. He has been called by a great English critic the last of the classics. The French writers of that epoch were misled by a wrong association of ideas and (as usual) by a perfect misunderstanding of the nature of English literature. Respect for truth, obedience to common sense, and observance of the canons of good taste, form no part of the French romantic revival. They are the very essence of the work of Sir Walter Scott.

Lockhart relates that Lord Cockburn, "when some glib youth chanced to echo in his hearing the consolatory tenet of local mediocrity, answered quietly—' I have the misfortune to think differently from you—in my humble opinion, Walter Scott's *sense* is a still more wonderful thing than his *genius*.'" And, writes Lockhart, "it was always Scott's favourite tenet, in contradiction to what he called the cant of sonneteers, that there is no necessary connection between genius and an aversion or contempt for any of the common duties of life; he thought, on the contrary, that to spend some fair portion of every day in any matter-of-fact occupation, is good for the higher faculties themselves in the upshot. In a word, from beginning to end, he piqued himself on being a man of business, and did—with one sad and memorable exception—whatever the ordinary course of things threw in his way, in exactly the businesslike fashion which might have been expected from the son of a thoroughbred old Clerk of the Signet, who had never deserted his father's profession."

It is Scott's strong grasp of the realities of life which endows his novels with the enduring quality of truth; the quality in which Dr Johnson, with his customary wisdom, affirmed to consist the chief value of any book. The same quality is inherent in Shakespeare, whose knowledge of law, of trade and commerce, of public affairs and the usages of the Court, so puzzles some of his commentators. The secret of the genius of Walter Scott is incommunicable. No one can explain how it is that from his easy, plain, and homely narrative is disengaged that peculiar poetic charm which escapes the utmost endeavours of other artists. But all can understand and admire and take as example the solid honest industry, the austere allegiance to duty, of Sir Walter. His countryman and disciple, Robert Louis Stevenson, was never more misguided than when he described Sir Walter as " a great romantic—an idle child." Stevenson wholly ignored the vast preparatory labours accomplished by Scott before he sat down to write; perhaps because Stevenson himself lacked that long preliminary discipline. Stevenson took great pains to achieve a technical perfection of style; and while it is in fact impossible to separate matter from manner, it is still true to say that if the work of Stevenson is more finely wrought, the work of Scott is infinitely the greater of the two.

But his poetic genius and his industry alone would not have served to achieve what Scott accomplished. The foundation of his greatness was morality.

The doctrine is none the less true because it is not fashionable. It is sometimes forgotten that although Walter Scott lived at a time of considerable licence, both in speech and in manners, there is not in the whole of his multitudinous works an offending word. His books, verse and prose alike, are the brave expression of courage, kindliness, mirth and beauty, chivalry and hardihood, virtue and a noble humanity. " God bless thee, Walter my man! Thou hast risen to be great, but thou wast always good," quoth his kinsman, the venerable Thomas Scott. In truth, Sir Walter rose to be great because he was good.

The episode of Melrose Abbey exemplifies Scott's method of work. They were the legends of Melrose which inspired Sir Walter Scott to write the two fine romances, *The Monastery* and its sequel *The Abbot*. The ruins of the great Cistercian monastery lay within a ride of his house at Abbotsford. Lockhart describes the view of Melrose beheld " aright " from the western turret of Abbotsford, " in the fair moonlight." " Nothing," writes Lockhart, " could be more lovely than the panorama; all the harsher and more naked features being lost in the delicious moonlight; the Tweed and the Gala winding and sparkling beneath our feet; and the distant ruins of Melrose appearing, as if carved of alabaster, under the black mass of the Eildons. The poet, leaning on his battlement, seemed to hang over the beautiful vision as if he had never seen it before." That was in 1818.

Four years later, in 1822, we find Scott, who had frequently pleaded with the Buccleuch family to preserve the ruins of Melrose, directing their repair and restoration on behalf of the young Duke of Buccleuch, to whom, under date May 15, 1822, he writes : " I am quite delighted with the commencement of the Melrose repairs, and hope to report progress before I leave the country, though that must be on Monday next. Please God, I will be on the roof of the old Abbey myself when the scaffolding is up." Lockhart records that the result of Sir Walter's restoration " was extremely satisfactory to all the habitual worshippers of these classical ruins."

Eight years later, in 1830, Scott wrote the introduction to *The Monastery*, in which, with his customary ingenuous and delightful candour, he tells his readers that he forgets why it was he chose " for the scene of his next attempt the celebrated ruins of Melrose, in the immediate neighbourhood of his own residence." The plan of the story of *The Monastery*, says Scott, was to exhibit the conflict of the two parties at the time of the Reformation, which should each " with the same sincerity and purity of intention, dedicate themselves, the one to the support of the sinking fabric of the [Roman] Catholic Church, the other to the establishment of the reformed doctrines . . . the ruins themselves form a splendid theatre for any tragic incident which might be brought forward. . . ."

In the " Introductory Epistle " prefixed to *The*

Monastery, Scott adapted the device of pretending that one Captain Clutterbuck (who succeeds Mr Jedediah Cleishbotham in the office) received the manuscript of the tale from a mysterious stranger, and that the Captain sought the aid of the author of *Waverley* in its editing and publication, tasks of which the worthy Captain, to his surprise, found himself incapable. Now, according to Captain Clutterbuck, the mysterious stranger, who was himself a disguised member of the Cistercian order, disinterred, with the Captain's assistance, a leaden casket from the ruins of Melrose. The manuscript confided by the stranger to Captain Clutterbuck, and by him to the author of *Waverley*, was to contain the history of the casket.

As a matter of fact it did not. For Scott wrote the " Introductory Epistle," all about Captain Clutterbuck and the priest and the discovery of the casket, before he wrote *The Monastery*, which history (he said) was contained in the priest's manuscript ; and although there is nothing about the casket in *The Monastery*, the author let his " Introductory Epistle " stand. In his introduction to its sequel, *The Abbot*, Sir Walter, with his charming candour aforesaid, confesses that when he came to write the two novels, he abandoned his original design.

Why did Scott abandon his original purpose? As Sir Walter does not care to tell us, let us refrain from inquiry.

Scott, consciously or unconsciously, believed that the relics of an heroic past were actually infused with the words and deeds of the men and women of departed generations. In 1818, the year in which Scott first dwelt in his new house at Abbotsford, the Regalia of Scotland were discovered. The barred chamber in the Castle of Edinburgh in which was the chest containing the Regalia, was opened in the presence of a Commission, of which Scott was a member. On the following day, February 5, 1818, " Scott and several of his brother commissioners revisited the Castle, accompanied by some of the ladies of their families. His daughter tells me," writes Lockhart, " that her father's conversation had worked her feelings up to such a pitch that when the lid was again removed, she . . . drew back from the circle. As she was retiring, she was startled by his voice protesting in a tone of the deepest emotion, ' something between anger and despair,' as she expresses it. One of the commissioners, not quite entering into the solemnity with which Scott regarded this business, had, it seems, made a sort of motion as if he meant to put the crown on the head of one of the young ladies near him, but the voice and aspect of the poet were more than sufficient to make the worthy gentleman understand his error ; and respecting the enthusiasm with which he had not been taught to sympathise, he laid down the ancient emblems with an air of . . . embarrassment." As well he might.

For Sir Walter's sentiment was more than enthusiasm. It was a passionate loyalty to the far-shining, immemorial goodness and greatness which none beheld more clearly, none more admirably depicted, than Sir Walter Scott.

Indeed, the present writer is prepared to maintain a theory that Scott was in fact gifted in a high degree with what he would have called second sight, and which to-day is called clairvoyance. The men and women whose characters he delineated, the scenes and events he depicted, were not the laborious creations of the intellectual faculty : they were beheld in a vision. Scott had access to what (for want of a better) is defined as the Universal Memory. He was at times wholly unconscious of what he was writing. His sufferings from the seizure of severe pain with which he was occasionally afflicted did not interrupt his work. During one such attack, when the pain was so sharp that it wrung groans even from the stoical Scott, as, unable to remain still, he writhed upon a couch, he dictated an entire novel. When he had recovered from his malady, he had no recollection of what he had done, and he read the manuscript with interest. He said he thought it was pretty good.

If, according to the suggested theory, communication was established between the mind of the author and unseen intelligences, it would be reasonable to suppose that the intelligences—or the Universal Memory—would reveal, not necessarily what had actually happened in the past, but their recollections of what happened ; and, further, that such memories would be coloured, as in life, by individual tendencies and predilections. Again, it is equally reasonable to suppose that these communications, upon passing into the author's mind, would there be modified to attune with his own conscious knowledge and ideas. And the total result would be in fact the novels of Sir Walter Scott. Like the work of all great men, it is unequal. There are passages in which the artist, lacking inspiration, is plainly getting on with the story by virtue of his acquired skill in carpentry. And there are passages—whole books, even—which excite the reader to cry, like Whyte Melville, Here is the God Almighty of novelists! In these masterpieces the reader is not only persuaded of their veracity, but he is aware of that strange enchanted atmosphere—vaguely called romantic, but it is not that—as of another and a more ethereal world, of which Scott is the magician. Compare his novels with the most finished and elaborate work of any other artist dealing in the same material, and the distinction becomes instantly vivid. Indefatigable and conscientious workman as he was, Scott seldom revised what he had written. Why not? Perhaps he felt that the inspiration was final, and the lack of it also final.

Examine the Scott manuscripts: the square pages, close-written from edge to edge, with scarce an erasure. There is a reminiscence somewhere recorded of a party of young men who were wont to assemble in a room in Edinburgh whose window looked across to the window of the room in which Sir Walter sat writing. They watched the strong hand moving steadily across the lamp-lit page, hour after hour, pausing only to turn over the written leaf. . . .

There is here at least a suggestion of what we call to-day automatic writing. It is of course easy to push an hypothesis too far. But it is probable that the quality called genius will presently be discovered in relation to more worlds than one.

JOHN CROME

JOHN CROME, the founder of the great
Norwich School of English painting, despite
the necessity of doing much drudgery to earn
his livelihood, became a master in his art. Known
and praised among painters in his time, Crome
won a fame which the years do but confirm.
Briefly, his life is an example of the steady turning
of all adverse circumstances to the achievement of
one supreme end.

John Crome was the son of a journeyman
weaver, who was also an innkeeper in a poor
quarter of the city of Norwich, and who was
registered as paying a rent of £5 a year, equiva-
lent to about £20 at the beginning of the present century. In the modern sense, young John
received no education at all. He was a sturdy,
cheery lad, as we gather from the little recorded
of his boyhood. When he was twelve years
of age, young John fell in with the other boys
and girls of his age, who assembled in the
open space in the city—the site of the vanished
Palace—to be hired into service. That ancient
custom in our day savours a little of slavery, but
it was not so regarded in 1780. A doctor, one
Edward Rigby, engaged John Crome as errand
boy. John seems to have been an enterprising
errand boy; for he used to prescribe for his

master's patients when the doctor was out of the way; and on one occasion he bled a man nearly to death. Dr Rigby, however, kept the lad for two years, and then helped to apprentice him to "a coach, house, and sign painter," Mr Francis Whisler, who abode at 41 Bethel Street, Norwich.

In those days, and for long afterwards, indentures of apprenticeship were extremely uncompromising instruments. The law did in fact deliver the hapless apprentice wholly to the will of his master for seven years. If the master were a good man, well; if not, it was very far from well. Of Mr Whisler's treatment of John Crome no record remains, but there is reason to suppose that John was contented enough, for at the expiration of his apprenticeship he continued to work for Whisler as his journeyman.

While he was still an apprentice, Crome became acquainted with another young gentleman of like tastes, Robert Ladbroke, who was apprenticed to a printer, Mr White. Now the printer, in his spare time, was an amateur of the arts, and painted landscape. It may be that he inspired his apprentice; at any rate, young Ladbroke proposed to become a painter. So did his friend John Crome: not a coach, house, and sign painter, but a real artist. The two lads, it is said, put their money together, hired an attic to serve for what was then called a painting-room, and purchased prints, which they used to copy for their edification. Crome's apprenticeship expired in 1790. At some time, probably a few months afterwards, he left Mr Whisler's service; and, with Ladbroke, commenced on his own account. He is said to have decorated sugar-cakes with ornamental devices. He painted several signboards, two of which remain.

The impression disengaged by the few facts known is that Crome cheerfully took any job that came along, lived as best he might, and doggedly continued to improve himself in his art. Besides the work by which he earned a little money, Crome produced sketches, and what in those days were known as compositions, which were exhibited in the shop windows of Messrs Smith and Jaggers, print-sellers at Norwich. At that period, side by side with the mass of ignorance, the sinister growth of the black manufacturing towns, the wild sports and brutal pastimes of the age, there beaconed among the aristocracy and the wealthier middle class the light of the true appreciation of art, and a high degree of education. Men who loved beautiful things were willing to pay for them. There were even rich men who understood that the pursuit of art and the gaining of money were commonly incompatible with each other. Hence, that invaluable institution, the Patron, who, in the case of John Crome, was Mr Thomas Harvey, of Catton, near Norwich.

Harvey invited Crome to his fine house at Catton, and made him free of his collection of pictures, among which were a Hobbema and a Gainsborough. There was then much communication between Eastern England and the Low Countries. Harvey himself had married a Dutch lady, and it is probable that his collection included the works of the famous Dutch painters. Here, then, was Crome's opportunity for the study of the masters of painting. Harvey introduced Crome to William Beechey, A.R.A.,[1] who invited the young man to visit him in London. It seems that Crome worked in Sir William's painting-room under his instruction, for Beechey records that "his visits were very frequent, and all his time was spent in my painting-room, when I was not particularly engaged. He improved so rapidly that he delighted and astonished me." Sir William also notes that Crome "was a very awkward, un-informed country lad, but extremely shrewd in all his remarks upon art, though he wanted words and terms to express his meaning."

Such, then, was Crome's education in art. In 1792, behold John Crome married, and earning his immediate livelihood as a drawing-master in Norwich. In those days, and for long afterwards, it was a part of the education of young ladies to acquire a certain proficiency in the use of what was elegantly termed "the pencil." The drawing-master arrived alternately with the dancing-master, and both these artists were expected to ring the bell at the servants' entrance and to dine in the servants' hall.

Crome built up a profitable practice, keeping two horses and riding upon his rounds, as he called them. In 1798, Crome was privileged to instruct the seven daughters of Mr John Gurney,

[1] Afterwards Sir William Beechey, R.A.

of Earlham. John Opie, A.R.A., who was painting subject-pictures and portraits, married a friend
of the Misses Gurney, and thus the two painters
became acquainted. Mrs Opie records that her
husband used to help Crome with the figures in
his landscapes ; for Crome had never gone through
the course of study of the antique and of the life,
which would have enabled him to draw the figure.
But by this time he was painting his magnificent
landscapes, and exhibiting many pictures annually
at Norwich, and some at the Royal Academy.

In 1813, Crome was appointed drawing-master
at Norwich Grammar School. Among his pupils
were George Borrow, and that strange adventur-
ous person who was to become Rajah Brooke of
Sarawak. Borrow did for Crome what one artist
could for another. In *Lavengro* he writes : " A
living master? Why, there he comes! Thou hast
had him long; he has long guided thy young
hand toward the excellence which is yet far from
thee, but which thou canst attain, if thou shouldst
persist and wrestle, even as he has done amid
gloom and despondency—ay, and even contempt
. . . the little stout man whose face is very dark,
and whose eye is vivacious . . . the little dark
man with the brown coat and the top boots, whose
name will one day be considered the chief orna-
ment of the old town, and whose works will at no
distant period rank among the proudest pictures of
England—and England against the world !—thy
master, my brother, thy, at present, all-too-little
considered master—Crome."

Borrow had an eye in his head; his rapid sketch of the man is good enough; and his prophecy came true. But it remains a mystery how Crome, who received no formal training, and who knew nothing of schools of art, achieved the mastery of his profession. In truth, it seems you may give a lad every advantage and he will do nothing with it; or you may give him nothing and he will do everything.

COMMERCIALISM AND ART

～

WHEN Colonel Newcome learned of his son's determination to be a painter, the good old soldier, too kind to quarrel with Clive, was saddened and disappointed; while Clive's grand relations frankly regarded the young man as lost to society. In those days of the early nineteenth century—say a hundred years since— it was not, you observe, respectable to be an artist. Art was not a profession. The Church and the Army: these were the respectable occupations. So was the Navy; but people seldom thought about the Royal Navy. One did not, unless they were the fashionable few, receive the members of the learned professions. Nevertheless, the making of money was also a highly respectable calling, always provided that you made enough money. Nobody thought the less of young Barnes New-come because he went to the City every morning. Banking—what could be more solid, more laud-able, more enviable, than that golden trade?

But a painter was associated with irregular hours, eccentric clothing, and the wearing of a beard. He was always impecunious, and who could wonder at it? Thus decreed that British society of which William Makepeace Thackeray has left so lively a record.

Now by virtue of a curious anomaly, that very

time was presently to bring forth painters whose achievement is second to none in the world. The mid-nineteenth century was a great and a prosperous age in painting. Society or no society, there grew and flourished a taste for works of art. These were the days of Flaxman, David Wilkie, Henry Raeburn, William Mulready, Charles Robert Leslie, William Etty, John Constable, Edwin Henry Landseer, William Clarkson Stanfield, Daniel Maclise, David Roberts, Thomas Creswick, John Phillip, Augustus Leopold Egg, Charles West Cope; men whose noble pictures remain in the national collections.

These artists, and many others, painted with the comfortable assurance that they would sell their work for good prices. A painter of merit did not lack commissions. The intelligent public had plenty of money and were ready to spend it upon what Mr Ruskin has nobly defined as the true wealth of a nation.

It was the fashion to buy what are called subject-pictures: representations of scenes or incidents, in which a story was told or suggested. The fashion has gone out now, and it is often condemned by the amateur critics, who, for reasons unknown, have invented a maxim that it is wrong for a painter to depict anything in the nature of a story. It is the fact, however, that during this period work was accomplished which all who love painting know to be the best of its kind.

Honour is due to the Prince Consort, who did all in his power to help and encourage every form of art. It was largely owing to the Prince that, when the new Houses of Parliament were being erected, painters were invited to compete for the internal decoration of that magnificent building. Among the successful competitors were Charles West Cope, William Dyce, and Daniel Maclise; and there can be no better example to the young artist of the deeds of his forefathers than the frescoes and wall-paintings in the Palace of Westminster.

About 1880 and onwards there came a change. People suddenly left off buying subject-pictures. Many an ambitious young painter was reduced to poverty. Nor has the subject-picture, save in a few cases, yet revived. The great historical picture was no longer painted, because no one would commission the artist. Painters had recourse to illustrative work in black-and-white; and those who possessed the requisite ability, and who found clients, painted portraits. There was more than one cause for the change, but the main cause may be defined in one word: commercialism.

Briefly described, what happened was the rise of the supremacy of the picture-dealer. From buying the pictures of living artists at a fair price, and reselling them to his customers at a reasonable profit, the picture-dealer evolved the brilliant idea of buying the pictures of dead artists extremely cheap and selling them extremely dear. Thus began that iniquitous traffic in what the dealers call Old Masters (real or spurious) which is associated with so many dubious transactions, and which is supported by so much revolting imposture.

In order to make the business both safe and profitable, it was first of all necessary to excite a demand on the part of the credulous public. The dealers, with all the traders' cunning, combined for the common purpose, and persuaded the public that to buy Old Masters was, above all, a sound investment. The deal had nothing to do with art except that art was used as a disguise. These tradesmen pointed to the prices fetched by this, that, and the other venerable, and very often ugly, masterpieces; but they omitted to mention that, as the aforesaid prices were fixed by the ring, or combine, which consisted of themselves, so they could (and did) *un*fix prices at any moment. The dealers, in a word, made and kept a market in Old Masters, exactly as middlemen make and keep a market in any other article.

By deliberately causing an artificial scarcity of the works of any given artist of the past, they forced up the price. It was paid because the purchaser believed it would continue to rise. Sometimes, of course, the collector would buy because he really believed he was purchasing a real work of art; and sometimes, but not often, he actually did obtain a fine work of art. Many hundreds of thousands of pounds thus merrily changed hand; English art was starving and neglected; and the system may be observed in operation to-day.

In the meantime, another blow fell upon the

artist. The development of photography and the invention of the process block put out of employment the artists who were drawing on wood for illustration, and therewith the wood-engravers also. The fine illustrative work of Millais, Creswick, Cope, Gilbert, Fildes, and other consummate artists ended. Steel-engraving went out. In the beautiful illustrated books and magazines of the nineteenth century there survive the examples of a lost art.

But commercialism did more than destroy. It built up. We are contemplating that edifice to-day, and the spectacle is far from encouraging. The dealers, for purposes of advertisement, associated with their operations writers in the Press who called themselves art critics. In truth, they knew nothing of criticism and less of art. They knew, however, the commercial value of pretence. Thus the dealers contrived an organization which could be employed for making known the works of certain men, which, in default of that machinery, would have remained unnoticed. Hence it is that the public are confused by eulogies of productions which are called by all sorts of queer names, such as Cubist, Futurist, Pointilliste, and so forth, or which are recommended simply because they differ from other representations in that they resemble no known object. But the authors of these abortions make their little arrangements with the professional art critics; who, by reason of some singular obliquity on the part of quite honest editors, are allowed to masquerade as authorities. The public, knowing nothing of the real character of their transactions, are sometimes deceived. More often they are disgusted. For commercialism has arrived by the road of mercenary advertisement at its logical development, the production of the ugly. That commercialism describes the ugly as beautiful, alters neither the nature of the thing described nor the right intuition of the public.

II : *BOOKS*

THE CAMBRIDGE SHAKESPEARE

IN the Cambridge University Press edition of the works of Shakespeare, we have—and the world has—for the first time, what may be called the definitive, or ultimate, or standard text. For here are gathered together, classified, analysed and sifted the vast collections of all previous editors in the light of the discoveries of researches which, it seems, leave very little else to discover, and certainly nothing material.

Now Sir Edward Maunde Thompson, who in 1916 published his book on *Shakespeare's Handwriting*, claims that there are extant (in the manuscript play *Sir Thomas More*) three pages in the handwriting of Shakespeare; and even if that eminent scholar should prove to be mistaken, there is no doubt whatever that the hand is of the same kind as that in which the six extant Shakespearean signatures are written.

The importance of this discovery consists in the ability it confers upon the student to trace the origin of the many doubtful words and obvious mistakes occurring in the first printed editions— the quartos—to the character of the poet's handwriting; for it is possible to write the same kind of hand to-day; and in so doing to perceive what letters may be mistaken by the compositor for other letters.

"The basis of the whole business," writes the textual editor of the Cambridge University Press edition, "in short, is the handwriting of Shakespeare; and that it is now possible not only to imagine but actually to write this hand is due to the researches of Sir Edward Maunde Thompson."

Shakespeare wrote what is called the English hand, which broadly speaking is German script, in contradistinction to the Italian hand, which is our script of to-day; and in the English hand, many letters are so nearly identical that, written carelessly, they are indistinguishable from one another.

Here, then, we have the solid foundation upon which the latest edition of Shakespeare is built. It is edited by Sir Arthur Quiller-Couch and Professor Dover Wilson. The volumes are admirably printed and bound, convenient for the pocket, and of a moderate price. In the first volume, *The Tempest*, Sir Arthur Quiller-Couch writes a general introduction, and an introduction to the play itself; Professor Dover Wilson writes the textual introduction. There are brief notes printed at the end, and a glossary. There is a facsimile of a page of the Shakespeare handwriting in *Sir Thomas More*. The little book, in a word, is a masterpiece of taste and scholarship.

There are two other recent discoveries which have enabled the editors to produce a definitive edition. Mr A. W. Pollard has proved that the first editions of Shakespeare were usually set up from the prompt-copies of the theatre; and "that many of these are likely to have been in the author's autograph; and that, therefore, the first editions of Shakespeare's plays—the quartos in particular—possess a much higher authority than editors have hitherto been inclined to allow them."

And Mr Percy Simpson, who published his *Shakespearean Punctuation* in 1911, and whose researches have been continued by Mr Pollard, has proved that "the stops in the folios and quartos . . . are now seen to be not the haphazard peppering of ignorant compositors, as all previous editors have regarded them, but playhouse punctuation, directing the actors how to speak their lines."

Both these discoveries accord with the known facts that Shakespeare was a practical playwright, writing wholly for the theatre. Many years of labour have been bestowed upon the minute analysis of the text of Shakespeare by the learned, who have rather ignored the conditions under which he worked, and tended (perhaps unconsciously) to assume that the poet wrote directly for publication and corrected his proofs in the modern manner. These labours have their own value; but in the circumstances they lead and can lead nowhither; unless, indeed, it may be said that by a process of elimination, and by the maintenance of steady research, they made possible the return to reality of the latest explorers.

Indeed, it is obvious to the student that the Cambridge University Press edition does in fact

abolish and sweep into limbo a whole library of
Shakespearean notes, annotations, various readings,
emendations, angry arguments, theories, conjectures ; and particularly and especially, as one hopes,
that unfortunate, ugly, and purely hypothetical
reconstruction of the poet's private life out of evidence gratuitously assumed by commentators to
be contained in his published works. Sir Arthur
Quiller-Couch, with his admirable taste and customary good sense, observes that " we should be
cautious, too, in listening to those who, all so
variously, utilise the Sonnets to construct fancy
histories of Shakespeare's personal life and actual
experience . . . it is mere guess-work to say that
because Shakespeare writes this or that in ' Lear '
or the Sonnets, therefore this or that must have
happened in his private life to account for his
writing just so."

And Sir Arthur goes on to remark how very
much better than " to hunt down the man who
enjoined to be written over his grave, ' Good
friend, for Jesus sake forbear . . .,' " it is to try
to trace, in the sequence of his works, the poet's
development as an artist.

The right order, in time, of the plays is now,
broadly speaking, established. They fall into six
groups (briefly tabulated by Sir Arthur Quiller-
Couch) from before 1595 to 1595, then in a series
of sections covering two years, three years, and
three sections of four years each, respectively. *The
Tempest* comes in the last category. It is placed first
in the new edition, merely to preserve the original

sequence in the first editions, and the decision was surely right.

The new edition lifts from the central luminary many bushels of conscientious pedantry; and its editors nobly fulfil the true office of criticism, which is to quicken perception by interpretation. And incidentally, it falls to be observed what an extraordinary witness to the great qualities of the poet resides in the survival of his works as we know them. The playwright, writing often carelessly, often composing at great speed under pressure of circumstances, carries his manuscript (the ink scarce dried) to the theatre, where it is divided among the players, or each actor copies out his part. Then the original manuscript becomes the prompt copy, upon which emendations are scrawled, and from which lines and passages are deleted. The author himself takes no more interest in his manuscript. "The copyright (as we call it) of his plays belonged to the theatre or Company for which they were written: and he never troubled himself or anybody to collect, correct, and print them. They were first gathered and given to the world by two fellow-actors, John Heminge and Henry Condell, late in 1623, or more than seven and a half years after his death."

In despite, then, of all neglect, indifference, chance and change and printers' errors, Shakespeare remained, and still remains, indestructible; in despite, also, of generations of critics and commentators and schoolmasters, the plays and poetry of Shakespeare are still the dearest and most delightful heritage of English-speaking people. And here might not one enter a plea for the hapless students of English literature who, in some universities (though not at Cambridge), are still required to learn by rote an interminable waste of bootless lore about Shakespeare, to the almost complete obscuration of the splendour, passion, beauty, and jollity of the plays themselves? After all, the most of Shakespeare is authentic enough ; if in the play the effect which the playwright intended to achieve, is achieved, it suffices ; and the rest (if one may dare to say so) does not, in fact, very much matter.

And it is the peculiar and shining merit of the editors of the Cambridge Shakespeare that their labours are directed to making the effect intended by the playwright as perfect as possible.

THE ENGLISH PICARESQUE NOVEL

⤮

THAT learned and witty doctor of medicine, Tobias George Smollett, writing in the mid-eighteenth century, reflected both the rough-spoken, heavy-fisted, brutal aspects of the age, and the sound learning, wit, observation, and astonishing vigour which were the attributes of the men of his day.

In 1748, when he had failed to prosper in his profession, Smollett published *The Adventures of Roderick Random*, which founded a new tradition of the English novel. That tradition was already flourishing abroad; and to Smollett belongs the achievement of completely expressing the foreign form in English terms. In 1594, Thomas Nash had published *The Unfortunate Traveller, or The Life of Jack Wilton*, whose ancestor, again, was the Spanish novel *Lazarillo de Tormes*, which had appeared some forty years before Nash's work. These were by no means the only examples of their kind; neither of them is of any great merit; but they emerge from the rest by reason of their typical construction, which set a fashion. The fashion became a tradition, which endures to this day; the tradition of the *novela picaresca*, the picaresque novel.

Beginning with *Lazarillo de Tormes* in Spain,

with *Jack Wilton* in English, it came to its full flower in France with the *Gil Blas* of Le Sage, published in 1735, and in England, thirteen years later, with *Roderick Random*. The picaresque novel, then, of which the early French model is *Gil Blas*, and the early English model is *Roderick Random*, is the story of the wandering, needy, shifty, not too scrupulous hero seeking his fortune; the novel which is constructed not upon a plot or pattern, but upon a succession of incidents cunningly woven in series. Smollett himself defines the method as the construction of "a large diffused picture, comprehending the characters of life, disposed in different groups and exhibited in various attitudes, for the purposes of an uniform plan." Which plan, he continues, "cannot be executed with propriety, probability, or success, without a principal personage to attract the attention, write the incidents, unwind the clue of the labyrinth, and at last close the scene, by virtue of his own importance."

Smollett's definition might loosely comprehend the English novel proper: but, when he wrote, the true indigenous English novel was then in the making, and the maker was Henry Fielding, whom Smollett both admired and hated. Smollett's models were in fact the French *Gil Blas*, and, to a lesser degree, *Don Quixote*, which he translated. But the difference between the French method and the English is extreme. In his essay upon Smollett, W. E. Henley admirably touches the distinction.

"Writing angrily and truculently where Le Sage had written with an urbane and intelligent smile; writing, too, with an utter contempt for the good taste, the good breeding, the reticence, the ironical and far-reaching amenity which, as being essentials in the great tradition of French literature, were so to say inherent in Le Sage, he set forth, so he avers, 'to represent modest merit'—in the person of Roderick Random!— 'struggling with every difficulty to which a friendless orphan is exposed, from his own want of experience, as well as from the selfishness, envy, malice, and base indifference of mankind.' Here, in other words, was the *novela picaresca* adapted to English uses and turned to English ends; and Le Sage himself, through whom its achievement was made possible, must certainly, could he have read, have been constrained to smile approval on the event."

Smollett, indeed, produced a model of its kind, in which every page, almost every sentence, is charged with life and action; and in which the characters (like them or dislike them as you may) are real people, delineated, not by means of analysis and descriptions, but by their own words and actions.

These, then, are the qualities which seized the imagination of the boy Charles Dickens, who became Smollett's greatest successor in his art. The evil in these wild books, as he tells us in *David Copperfield*, passed him by. He learned from Smollett, unconsciously, the method of the picaresque novel. It must be wrought about a central figure; it must be humorous or even farcical, and it might be sentimental; and it must be crammed with incident. So long as the narrative be consistent with itself, having a coherent beginning and a definite end, it will fulfil the purpose of its being, which (in a word) is to amuse.

To what excellent purpose the young man Charles Dickens turned the lessons of his rather sinister and far from amiable master, Mr Pickwick is there to prove. In *Pickwick* we have the English epic of kindly mirth : all the good of Smollett's admirable craftsmanship retained, all the bad discarded. Dickens possessed the skill, the invention, the humour, and the power of delineating character which were Smollett's; but he had more : he had the inestimable and shining gift of human sympathy; and he owned, what Smollett lacked, the quality which Henry James has described as the intense and far-reaching vision of the picturesque. From *Pickwick* he was to go forward to other and greater achievements of which Smollett was wholly incapable.

It should be noted, also, that *The Adventures of Sir Lancelot Greaves*, completed by Smollett in 1762, was published as a serial; and, says Mr Henley, it " may very well have been the first piece of fiction written in English to that end. Two of Defoe's—*Robinson Crusoe* (First Part) and *Captain Singleton*—had been so published, but both had existed for some time in book form." Now *Pickwick*, as every one knows, was also written as a serial; and in Dickens' time it became a customary mode of publication.

Not to mention the influence, which remains to this day, of Smollett's methods and Smollett's characters upon a host of other writers, it may be remarked that the great Sir Walter himself said that to Lismahago, the Lieutenant in *Humphry Clinker*, he owed something of his Dugald Dalgetty.

So true it is that a man knows not what he does; but if he does his best, he may rest assured the good in it will survive and fructify; and posterity, as Thomas Nash, himself an early amateur of the picaresque, recommended, may gather honey out of "the bitterest flowers and sharpest thistles."

The supreme example of picaresque honey is *David Copperfield*. Like *Pickwick*, and unlike the rest of Dickens' novels, it is woven upon no elaborate plot. The story turns about the central figure. Dickens was fond of devising an ingenious plot, which—one cannot but observe—he sometimes forgot in the delightful abundance of his creation. But in *David Copperfield* he discarded the fascinating element of mystery; bent the whole power of his immense genius upon the interplay of quaint and lovable character; and produced a masterpiece of the English picaresque. In *David Copperfield* the central figure is no longer, as in Le Sage and Smollett, an attractive scamp, keeping company with ruffians and wantons of various degree. The hero is a modest, amiable youth of the English middle class, whose friends are virtuous and kindly folk, and whose enemies, even, are respectable. The book is the epic of Victorian, domestic England, irradiated throughout by generous sentiment and honest affection, like the glow of firelight in a comfortable room in which familiar friends assemble. It is the peculiar glory of English letters that such a work should be both the achievement of a great artist and the expression of the national spirit, so that *David Copperfield* is a household possession.

In *Barry Lyndon* Thackeray wrote a picaresque novel in another manner. Here, the central figure is an adventurer devoid of morality and destitute of conscience, frequenting the worst company. The Irish despoiler Barry Lyndon is presented in terms of irony with so subtle a skill that the book is a masterpiece of its kind. Doubtless Thackeray learned somewhat from Henry Fielding's *Jonathan Wild*, itself a classic example of the ironical picaresque. But the element of irony is foreign to the English taste. The English public like plain dealing. If a malefactor annoys them, they like to see him knocked out with a blow on the point, and then to go on with their business.

A NOTE ON THE ROMANTIC

W HAT is Classic, and what Romantic?
Although an age-long controversy has
been waged about these innocent expressions, students of literature are still at a loss
to know what they really mean. For Classic is
commonly defined as opposed to Romantic, the
inference being that you may deal in one or the
other, but not in both at the same time. Whereas
the truth is there is no such contradiction, the
difference between the two being mainly a matter
of critical theory; for the spirit of both Classic
and Romantic art, rightly considered, is one and
the same; and that spirit is capable of an infinite
variety of expression.

Classic is the term that denotes the art of the
Ancients, the monuments in architecture, sculpture, and literature of the artists of Greece and of
Rome. The men of the Renaissance restored the
knowledge of Classic art to Europe; although, in
truth, it had never died, for the Classic literature
survived in every centre of learning. What the
men of the Renaissance really did was to fan these
smouldering embers into a noble radiance. And
here it falls to be remarked that there never was
anything more truly Romantic than the Classic art
of the Renaissance, unless it were the Classic art
itself. Nevertheless, in due time there emerged

a new manifestation, which was called Romance. And if at this point the bewildered student will hold fast to the truth that the same spirit wrought both Classic and Romantic, he will be enabled to resolve much confusion of thought. And he will be further consoled in remembering that to both Classic art and Romantic art the same criterion of merit is applied. There is but one criterion, which is good taste. The French define good taste as the opinion of the most intelligent people, expressed through a long period of time. And with that we must even be content.

What is called Romance has assumed many forms throughout the ages. The particular manifestation with which the present age is chiefly concerned, appeared in France in the eighteenth century. To-day, the word Romance is generally used to convey a variety of meanings. When a novel, or a play, or a person is called Romantic, the expression probably signifies the unusual, or the picturesque, or the sentimental, or the improbable, or all these. But the technical meaning of the word cannot be so easily defined. Perhaps it is insusceptible of exact definition.

In what Romance really consists may, however, be apprehended in the light of the history of what is portentously called the Romantic Movement in Literature. These words delight the professors of criticism. They affect the student with a sense of chill. He knows what they imply. They warn him that in order to pass examinations, he will be compelled to learn by heart a deal of tedious information concerning origins, and dates, and names of authors of whose books he has never heard, and does not desire to read, and disquisitions upon the influence of one writer upon another writer, of one School upon another School : every thing but the thing itself.

But let the student take courage. These professional classifications bear the same relation to literature as the botanists' catalogue bears to the bright and living beauty of the garden. There, the flower is the real thing. In literature, man is the real thing. For the book is the soul of a man. And the history of the Romantic movement in Literature does ultimately lead us to men. The professors very kindly show us the way to their houses.

Now the professors tell us that the word Romantic in the eighteenth century, alike in France, Germany, and England, simply meant ' barbarous.' So did the word Gothic. The French critics of the eighteenth century regarded Shakespeare as both barbarous and Gothic ; and by these expressions they meant, contrary to the rules of civilized art. It was during the eighteenth century that the word Romantic came to mean something very definite and very serious ; for it was used to define a new form of art, which, in one shape or another, remains with us to-day ; and which cannot be rightly estimated except in the knowledge of its origin.

There were two Romantic movements, as they were called : one in France, the other in England,

and each influenced the other; and each in its way was a revolution. Indeed, it is commonly said that the French Romantic movement in literature was one of the causes of that terrific catastrophe, the French Revolution. It was not. What happened was that the French Romantic writers expressed in their work some of the causes of the French Revolution. No writer, howsoever gifted, can make a political revolution all by himself, or even with the help of a few literary friends.

It is true to say, however, that the literature of to-day is largely built upon the foundation of the French Romantic movement. And it is all the more important to understand that movement, because in the state of Europe after the fall of the Napoleonic Empire there is a parallel to the state of Europe subsequent to the Great War. The Romantic movement triumphed after the fall of the Napoleonic Empire; and something of the same sort may be happening now. This at least may be said: that, as in the early nineteenth century all Europe was in confusion, and France suffered the decline of ancient tradition, and fell into disorder and bankruptcy, and yet in due season became more peaceful, stronger, and more prosperous than ever before; so in our generation, we may look forward to the same happy restoration.

Romanticism in France began before the French Revolution, endured throughout the Empire, and flourished after its fall. It was in part the expression of the sentiment of the time, and in part a new discovery in art. French art, until the years immediately preceding the French Revolution, was what is called Classic, which means the tradition of the Renaissance, itself the revival of the rules of art followed by the great masters of antiquity. These rules, according to the custom of the French, were carefully deduced from the works of the Classics. The whole of the art of the Middle Ages was dismissed as Gothic, barbarous, and unworthy of the attention of a polite people. So it was ordained that all art, whether literature or painting, sculpture or architecture, must be regulated by the rules of the Classic tradition. Prose must be written in a certain manner, or not at all. Verse must be strictly measured, or it was not verse. Certain subjects must be treated in prose; other subjects must be treated in verse; others, again, were considered outside the range of art altogether. The same rules applied to the arts other than the art of literature. Either they conformed to the rules attributed to Classic art, or they were nothing.

It seems that when a particular mode of art has been practised for a certain length of time, significance departs from it, and it becomes what is called conventional. It is perfectly correct; it observes all the rules; and yet nobody cares any more about it. That was the position in the mid-eighteenth century in France. It also seems that when such a position occurs, an artist almost always arises with a new idea. And in France he

is invariably treated as a dangerous rebel, so that
he is obliged desperately to fight for his idea.
For in France matters of art are regarded with
a gravity scarcely known in England. In England, these things are taken more easily. It is for
that reason the Romantic movement in France is
more vividly manifested than its counterpart in
England.

First of all, then, the French Romantic movement was a revolt—not against the Classic, as such,
but against the rules and conventions of the Classic
tradition. It coincided with that other revolt of
the time, the rebellion against the whole political
system, which was presently to be destroyed in the
Revolution.

After these tedious but necessary observations,
we arrive at the real origin of French Romanticism,
which was the man Jean Jacques Rousseau.

Rousseau was born in 1712. He published *La
Nouvelle Héloïse* in 1761. Bernardin de Saint-
Pierre, in some sort the disciple of Rousseau,
published his *Paul et Virginie* in 1787. Then
came the Revolution, and with it the sequestration
of literature. In 1800, Napoleon was First Consul,
and order was established. In 1801, François
Auguste René de Chateaubriand (born 1768)
published *Atala*, a part of his immense work *Les
Natchez*, which was composed in England. In
1810, Mme de Staël published her *De l'Allemagne*,
in which ingenious discourse upon German literature and art that eminent lady expounded the
method of French Romanticism, and so prepared

the way for the publication in 1826 of the whole of Chateaubriand's *Les Natchez*.

These, then, were the founders of the French Romantic movement. Rousseau has been called the grandfather, Chateaubriand the father, and Bernardin de Saint-Pierre the uncle, of the French Romantic movement. And of these Jean Jacques Rousseau has exercised the more enduring influence.

These men accomplished what was in fact the liberation of French literature from the outworn rules of convention drawn from the Classic tradition. In prose and verse alike they introduced new harmonies. As in all such new beginnings, the leaders of revolt, rejecting convention, returned to the direct observation of nature. For Rousseau's discovery of the Romantic consisted in his enthusiastic delineation of landscape and of natural objects—and of the natural mind of Rousseau himself in particular—drawn from the life as he saw them.

Instead of modelling his subject to accord with the Classic method of dealing with such material, Rousseau drew directly from nature. Thus Romanticism acquired one of its original qualities: the representation of ordinary experience intensified by emotion, as distinguished from the Classic representation, which by degrees had forgotten all about actual experience and was devoid of emotion.

And the French novelists of to-day are still influenced by the French Romantic movement of the early nineteenth century. They inherit a tradition very often without knowing it. During the last thirty or forty years, some of the English novelists have also learned at the same school, and perhaps, also, without quite understanding the lesson. Perhaps they have denied themselves the privilege of reading M. Lemaître's admirable study of Jean Jacques Rousseau, which would enlighten them.

M. Lemaître remarks that the work of Rousseau was a thing unique in literature. Indeed, Rousseau himself deliberately posed as the lonely prophet. He professed to make himself a place apart, in life and in literature. Not that he was really solitary, for he dwelt habitually in congenial society, preferably among the French aristocracy. He taught that man was formed to live alone; and none was so indignant as Rousseau when people took him at his word. He preached that all men were born equal, and he could never forget that he had been a lackey, nor refrain from admiring the condescension of men in high place. His ambition was to marry into a noble house.

These contradictions are significant. In truth, the life and work of Rousseau are one long contradiction. His theory and his practice were almost always opposed to each other. Few men succeed in harmonizing them completely, but Rousseau never. Whatever he did, produced the effect exactly opposite to the effect he intended.

When, for example, Rousseau, in 1753, wrote

his celebrated *Discourse upon the Origin and Foundations of Inequality among Mankind* his intention was to point the way to peace and happiness upon earth. What happened was that his eloquent phrases partly inspired the French Revolution and were employed by the revolutionaries in justification of the Terror. Marat used to declaim them in public. Any event more odious to Rousseau than the Revolution, which apparently he did not foresee, cannot be imagined. Again, in his treatise upon *The Social Contract* Rousseau's purpose was to found a new system of law and liberty based upon the will of the whole people. The result was a scheme which, in practice, would (and in fact did) produce the most dreadful form of tyranny. Rousseau himself, after some further reflections, remarked that he would prefer not only an absolute despotism, but something more than absolute, if such a thing could be.

Rousseau wrote his *Discourse upon Equality* in response to the public invitation of the Academy of Dijon, which set as the subject for an essay " What is the origin of inequality among mankind, and is it in accordance with the law of nature? " And he began his treatise by placidly announcing that he proposed to ignore all facts, because facts had nothing to do with the question. Rousseau preferred, he said, to rely upon hypothetical reasoning, which he regarded as the only instrument for discovering the real origin of things.

Rousseau, and his successors, insisted that their discoveries were just as true as facts ; that they were merely a different kind of fact. It may be admitted that the theory is confusing; but the French Romantic movement *is* confusing. Rousseau announced that he read the history of mankind, not in books, which were false, but in nature, which was infallible. What did he mean by nature? No one has ever been able to answer that question. But in practice what Rousseau meant by nature was his own nature; his own quivering, vivid, lascivious, and wandering fantasy.

Had Rousseau written only political treatises, it may be doubted if he would have founded the Romantic movement. But he wrote *La Nouvelle Héloïse*, *Émile*, the *Confessions*, and much more. And in these works, still proceeding upon his doctrine of disregarding every one except himself, he composed passages of so singular a merit and so admirable a beauty that they were a revelation in art. Here, again, Rousseau produced an effect he did not intend. His purpose was to prove with the utmost solemnity a moral proposition. The proposition itself was not (in fact) moral; and what the moralist actually accomplished was the delineation of new effects in a new manner. In a word, he set a fashion in art.

Of that fashion, there were many developments; but the Romantic influence survived through all vicissitudes, and survives to-day. If the student of French contemporary literature is puzzled (as well he may be) by works which seem to present no particular reason for their existence; which exhibit no plan, or plot; which are drenched in unwholesome sentiment, which obliterate morality, but which are charged with much admirable description and crowded with elaborate detail, he may turn to the troubled pages of Rousseau, and therein he will perceive the explanation, and much matter besides.

The first effect of the Romantic movement in England was the appearance of Samuel Richardson's *Clarissa Harlowe*; the long, excessively sentimental novel told in the form of letters, like *La Nouvelle Héloïse*. The mode for ' sensibility,' as it was called, in the eighteenth century in England, and since, was adopted from the French Romantics. The novels of Henry Fielding were a sturdy protest against the fashion; and they founded the sound tradition of the English novel. That tradition was nobly maintained by the great English novelists: by Tobias Smollett, Charles Dickens, William Makepeace Thackeray, George Eliot, Anthony Trollope, and the rest of the Victorian artists. They took from the French what seemed to them good, and left the rest aside.

But the contrast between the French and the English tradition of letters appears nowhere so vividly as in Thackeray's entertaining criticisms. In 1841, Thackeray lived in Paris, making his living by his pen. He wrote immensely: he wrote stories, essays, criticisms, descriptions of the life about him; and he wrote so wisely and wittily, that we can still read his account of the ephemeral doings of the day, with an added pleasure, the pleasure of contemplating vivid pictures of vanished things. Thackeray frequented the theatre, from which he derived an unfailing enjoyment, though it was not always, or even often, the kind of amusement the playwright and the players intended to provide.

During the fifty years which had elapsed since the death of Rousseau, the French Romantic school had found a new prophet in the great, the sublime Victor Hugo, who, like other prophets, had his rivals as well as his disciples. In 1830, Hugo had produced his *Hernani*, a tremendous drama which marked a revolution—in France it is always a revolution—in the art of the theatre.

Side by side with the new drama survived (as it still survives) the French classical tradition : the tradition of Racine, of Corneille, of Molière ; the classical tragedy and comedy. And there was also the perennial French farce, the Palais Royal entertainment. But let Mr Thackeray explain this matter in his own way. " There are three kinds of drama in France, which you may subdivide as much as you please. There is the old classical drama, well-nigh dead, and full time, too ; old tragedies, in which half-a-dozen characters appear, and spout sonorous Alexandrines for half-a-dozen hours. The fair Rachel has been trying to revive this *genre*, and to untomb Racine ; but be not alarmed, Racine will never come to life again, and cause audiences to weep as of yore. Madame Rachel can only galvanize the corpse, not revivify it. Ancient French tragedy, red-heeled, patched and be-periwigged, lies in the grave ; and it is

138

only the ghost of it that we see, which the fair Jewess has raised. There are classical comedies in verse too, wherein the knavish valets, rakish heroes, stolid old guardians, and smart free-spoken serving-women discourse in Alexandrines as loud as the Horaces or the Cid. An Englishman will seldom reconcile himself to the *roulement* of the verses, and the painful recurrence of the rhymes; for my part I had rather go to Madame Saqui's, or to see Deburau dancing on a rope: his lines are quite as natural and poetical.

" Then there is the comedy of the day, of which Monsieur Scribe is the father. Good heavens! with what a number of gay colonels, smart widows and silly husbands has that gentleman peopled the play-books! How that unfortunate seventh commandment has been maltreated by him and his disciples! . . .

" Finally, there is the Drama, that great monster which has sprung into life of late years, and which is said, but I don't believe a word of it, to have Shakespeare for a father. If Monsieur Scribe's plays may be said to be so many ingenious examples how to break one commandment, the *Drama* is a grand and general chaos of them all; nay several crimes are added, not prohibited in the Decalogue, which was written before dramas were."

In the *Tour de Nesle* Dumas the elder had done in another aspect of the romantic drama what Hugo had done with *Hernani*. Thackeray thus describes the works of the two great romantics:

"Of the drama, Victor Hugo and Dumas are the well-known and respectable guardians. Every piece Victor Hugo has written since *Hernani* has contained a monster—a delightful monster, saved by one virtue. There is Triboulet, a foolish monster; Lucrèce Borgia, a maternal monster; Mary Tudor, a religious monster; Monsieur Quasimodo, a humpbacked monster; and others that might be named, whose monstrosities we are induced to pardon—nay, admiringly to witness— because they are agreeably mingled with some exquisite display of affection. And, as the great Hugo has one monster to each play, the great Dumas has, ordinarily, half a dozen, to whom murder is nothing; common intrigue, and single breakage of the before-mentioned commandment, nothing; but who live and move in a vast, delightful complication of crime that cannot be easily conceived in England, much less described. . . .

" Or, to speak more seriously, and to come, at last, to the point. After having seen most of the grand dramas which have been produced in Paris for the last half dozen years, and thinking over all that one has seen—the fictitious murders, rapes, adulteries, and other crimes, by which one has been interested and excited—a man may take leave to be heartily ashamed of the manner in which he has spent his time; and of the hideous kind of mental intoxication in which he has permitted himself to indulge. . . .

"Let us leave plays," Thackeray continues, " for a moment, for poetry, and take an instance of French criticism concerning England from the works of a French exquisite and man of letters . . . Monsieur Roger de Beauvoir, a gentleman who actually lived many months in England, as an attaché to the embassy of M. de Polignac. He places the heroine of his tale in a *petit réduit près le Strand*, ' with a green and fresh jalousie, and a large blind, let down all day; you fancied you were entering a bath of Asia, as soon as you had passed the perfumed threshold of this charming retreat ' ! He next places her

> Dans un square écarté, morne et couvert de givre,
>   Où se cache un hôtel, aux vieux lions de cuivre ;

and the hero of the tale, a young French poet, who is in London, is truly unhappy in that village.

> Arthur dessèche et meurt.   Dans la ville de Sterne,
>   Rien qu'en voyant le peuple, il a le mal de mer ;
> Il n'aime ni le Parc, gai comme une citerne,
>   Ni le tir au pigeon, ni le *soda-water*.[1]
>
>   .   .   .   .   .
>
> Et chaque gentleman lui dit : L'heureux poète !

' L'heureux poète ' indeed ! I question if a poet in this wide world is so happy as M. de Beauvoir, or has made such wonderful discoveries. ' The bath of Asia, with green jalousies,' in which the lady dwells ; ' the old hotel, with copper lions, in a lonely square ';—were ever such things heard of, or imagined, but by a Frenchman? . . . And this gentleman has lived for many months amongst us ; admires *Williams Shakspear*, the

[1] The italics are the poet's own.

141

' grave et vieux prophète,' as he calls him, and never, for an instant, doubts that his description contains anything absurd ! "

Thackeray, in dealing with the French novel, is not less illuminating. Those were the days of George Sand, Victor Hugo, Alexandre Dumas, Balzac, and of " a new writer, Monsieur de Bernard," passages from whose lively and satirical works Thackeray translates for his English readers. M. de Bernard's books are nearly forgotten, as, indeed, are the novels of the Frenchman's English contemporaries, Lady Morgan and Mrs Trollope. How little did their authors imagine that the writing of the tall young man with the eyeglass, who treated his eminent contemporaries with so ingenious a freedom, would survive all the caprices of fashion, which condemn so many masterpieces to oblivion !

Of " the fashionable part " of M. de Bernard's novels Thackeray writes : " Caricature as it is, we have an accurate picture of the actual French dandy. Bets, breakfast, riding, dinners at the ' Café de Paris,' and delirious Carnival balls : the animal goes through all such frantic pleasures at the season that precedes Lent. He has a wondrous respect for English ' gentlemen-sportsmen '; he imitates their clubs—their love of horseflesh : he calls his palefrenier a groom, wears blue bird's-eye neckcloths, sports his pink out hunting, rides steeple-chases, and has his Jockey Club. The ' tigers and lions ' alluded to in the report have been borrowed from our own country, and a great

compliment is it to M. de Bernard, the writer of
the above amusing sketch, that he has such a
knowledge of English names and things, as to give
a Tory lord the decent title of Lord Cobham, and
to call his dog O'Connell. Paul de Kock calls an
English nobleman, in one of his last novels, *Lord
Boulingrog*, and appears vastly delighted at the
verisimilitude of the title."

Quite unawares, Thackeray, in his sketches and
criticisms—which, outspoken as they are, never
fail of charity and magnanimity—reveals his own
delightful qualities. Thackeray never tries to be
clever ; he was content, as Lady Ritchie says somewhere, simply to express that which was in him.
Hence it is that in reading either his slightest
sketches or his more serious criticisms, the reader
discovers a delightful feeling that a genial, wise,
and humorous gentleman is talking to him with
the greatest courtesy and kindliness.

The French Romantics of 1840, whom
Thackeray limned in his immortal pages, had
their riotous day and so departed, giving place to
new men and new modes. It was but a mock
obeisance that was paid to the venerable Victor
Hugo at the last. The men of the years about
1840 drove their methods to the extreme of
absurdity ; and much of their work, condemned
by that good taste of intelligent people, of
which Thackeray was the English exponent, has
vanished into oblivion. That which is of per-
durable value remains ; and the student who
judges the achievement of the great Romantics

rather by what it really is than by the *catalogue raisonné* of the professors, will probably forget to distinguish between Classic and Romantic, in his admiration for the inexhaustible diversity and the ineluctable courage of the spirit of man.

VINTAGE NEW AND OLD

IT is the privilege of young men to be miserable
in print. Jaques the melancholy savoured that
affection with a perverted pleasure; but when
he was not in the mood, he was probably as
jolly a fellow as any in the woodland. Similarly,
when our commencing poets are not making portentous and terrifying verses, doubtless they are
perfectly cheerful, even (it may be) hilarious. As
they grow in years, so they come to perceive that
life is not in fact a witches' sabbath but something even pleasant; and they may also begin to
understand that poetry is not necessarily poetry
because it is framed in strange, rich, and exotic
terminology.

It is of course possible to account for the gloom
of the youthful poet by calling it a phase, as the
saying is, through which he must pass to attain
to brighter things. Indeed, it may be so. At the
same time, it falls to be observed that it is really
easier, especially in the case of young people
highly gifted with imagination, to be sad than to
be merry. It does not, however, follow that sad-
ness makes a work of art, nor that the easier task
is the right task. And what are we to think of
young gentlemen who first construct a series of
impossible situations, and then proceed to indite an
elaborate series of verses in which they agonizingly

describe themselves as enduring the most frightful emotions? For that the events thus pictured
really happened, or could happen, the reader cannot believe.

Mr Robert Nichols, for instance, in his book
of verse, *Aurelia and other Poems*, publishes a
series of twenty-seven sonnets, in the manner of
the late William Shakespeare. Now if we applied
to the sonnets of Mr Nichols the method applied
by the critics to the sonnets of Shakespeare, and
endeavoured to discover therein evidence of the
poet's own experience in his private life, it could
only be said that the results could not be set
down, because they would be libellous. They
would also be absurd. Shakespeare is dead, and
therefore defenceless. Mr Nichols (happily) is
neither. Yet he writes:

> Still shall the World-to-come our love review,
>   Dissect my pain and analyse your pride,
> Dispute our deeds and their complexions' hue,
>   And over our right and wrong wrongly divide.

Yes, but will it? One thinks not. One certainly hopes not. And when we find Mr Nichols
making so ingenious a series of sonnets—and
he has not gone to school to the late William
Shakespeare entirely without profit—we begin to
think that the vast critical apparatus concerning
Shakespeare and the Dark Lady and Mr W. H.
and all the rest of it means nothing and is nothing.
Very likely Shakespeare, like other young men,
and like (as one believes) Mr Nichols, was trying

an experiment in the fashionable mode of the sonnet; in which case Shakespeare's gentle spirit would have been pleasantly amused by the immense and futile toils of the critics; who, instead of attending to the poetic effect for which Shakespeare strove, and which he now and again so superbly achieved, insist on groping for a meaning which is not there.

But ingenious craftsman as Mr Nichols is, so that he can imitate to a hair the very trick of the Elizabethans, he does not always write poetry. For instance, the second sonnet, *To Aurelia*:

> Seeing your eyes I know where sorrow is,
>> So steadfastly they contradict your youth,
> So ag'd a blue tincts their drugged irises,
>> So blank are the pupils fixed on deadly truth.
> Who gave you these most terrible of eyes,
>> That never, never, never know to weep,
> That have become my life's unpitying spies,
>> Nor sleep themselves nor suffer me to sleep?

It is all there—all, except the one thing essential, which (for want of a better) we call poetry. Again, in *The Deliverer*, there are skill in epithet, vivid fancy, and picturesque phrase, but not poetry. It is a narrative; and narrative in verse is always hard to handle; and why should the poet be at the pains to deal in ugliness and squalor, especially when the truth of the picture is singularly dubious?

Of another quality is Mr Robert Graves, who, in his *Fairies and Fusiliers*, thus disarms

147

the "ungentle critic" in the first poem in the book:

> You'll only frown; you'll turn the page,
>   But find no glimpse of your New Age
> Of Poetry in my worn-out words. . . .
> No, no! my chicken, I shall scrawl
>   Just what I fancy as I strike it,
> Fairies and Fusiliers, and all.
>   Old broken knock-kneed thought will crawl
> Across my verse in the classic way.
>   And, Sir, be careful what you say;
> There are old-fashioned folk still like it.

There are indeed, the present writer among them: among the old-fashioned folk who flatter themselves they know the real thing when they see it. How hearty a piece is *The Legion*, in which Strabo and Gracchus are limned taking their wine, and watching the new men of the Legion marching by. The old centurion is appalled by their unsoldierly aspect. But, quoth Gracchus:

> The Legion is the Legion while Rome stands,
>   And these same men before the autumn's fall
> Shall bang old Vercingetorix out of Gaul!

As indeed we know they did! And here is the charming opening to *Babylon*:

> The child alone a poet is:
>   Spring and Fairyland are his.
> Truth and Reason show but dim,
>   And all's poetry with him.
> Rhyme and music flow in plenty
>   For the lad of one-and-twenty. . . .

And how pleasant is *The Cottage*. Here is no picture of weeping rain and misted fields and squalor, so beloved of the young poets, when they happen to leave London for a few days, but :

> Here in turn succeed and rule
> Carter, smith and village fool.
> Then again the place is known
> As tavern, shop and Sunday-school ;
> Now somehow it's come to me
> To light the fire and hold the key,
> Here in Heaven to reign alone.
>
> All the walls are white with lime,
> Big blue periwinkles climb
> And kiss the crumbling window-sill ;
> Snug inside I sit and rhyme,
> Planning poem, book, or fable,
> At my darling beech-wood table
> Fresh with bluebells from the hill. . . .

In a word, Mr Robert Graves can, and does, write poetry which is poetry. How is it done? Nobody knows. But when it is done, you can recognize it. And among the marks of the real thing are a brave and an honest spirit, a love of the beautiful, a delight in laughter, and a sense of music in the use of words. Even so, there remains a mysterious element which we cannot define. Sir Henry Newbolt once called it the poet's " bonus." Signor Benedetto Croce (the Bergson of criticism) calls it "intuition." Does that help us? Not very much. However, there it is ; and for that let us give praise.

A QUESTION OF CONSCIENCE

THERE are of course many private letters which, dealing with matters not demanding reticence, are of a nature to enrich literature. Nor is it difficult to decide between what may and what may not be made known; for the test to be applied is the feeling on the subject of the writer of the letters. He (or she) is entitled to the most scrupulous consideration, whether it be during his life or after his death. There is a noble curiosity concerning the lives of the great, which endeavours to learn what they did, and how they did it. And there is an ignoble curiosity to which nothing is sacred; and which is never tired of constructing what are often malign theories out of the very orts and heeltaps of gossip.

Thackeray, a sensitive and a high-minded man, forbade the publication of his remains. Shakespeare left an injunction to "forbear," which has been observed in the letter but not in the spirit. Oliver Goldsmith destroyed his papers. But no man can ensure that his correspondents will either destroy his letters or preserve their secrets.

It was not until 1920 that the original manuscripts of the Vanessa correspondence were discovered, and were purchased by the British Museum. For the first time, then, the letters

were edited from the originals, by Mr A. Martin
Freeman, with a scholarship and a discretion
which in this case were peculiarly needed. For
none, perhaps, has suffered so rudely from the
shameless hand of posterity as the late Dean
Swift: the melancholy, angry, proud man who
so fiercely resented the world's meddling with
his private affairs. It is sure that had Swift foreseen, for instance, the publication of his correspondence with Miss Esther Vanhomrigh, the
Dean's wrath would have found devastating expression. But the harm was done long ago. The
letters were published in Sir Walter Scott's edition
of Swift's complete works of 1814; and they are
included in the six volumes of Swift's correspondence edited by Dr Elrington Ball. Mr Freeman's
volume is entitled *Vanessa and her Correspondence
with Jonathan Swift*.

Vanessa, of course, is Esther Vanhomrigh,
whose surname was pronounced, according to an
eighteenth-century commentator, "Vannummery."
In the poem addressed to the lady by Dean Swift,
the Dean named his friend Vanessa and himself
Cadenus, an anagram of Decanus, or Dean.

Esther, or Hester, Vanhomrigh was the eldest
daughter of Mrs Vanhomrigh, a cheerful widow;
who, when Swift made her acquaintance, was living in London on a small fortune. Swift became
a friend of the family; and in 1711 he was their
constant guest. The great wit, writer, and politician felt pity and affection for the girl whom, he
thought, he could help and guide in the cultivation

of her rare abilities. Thus began the friendship between Swift and Vanessa.

Swift was one of the great letter-writers of literature: easy, witty, vivid, and poignant. In his letter to Miss Anne Long, of December 18, 1711, Swift, referring to his young pupil Esther, writes: " I think there is not a better girl upon earth. I have a mighty friendship for her. She has good principles, and I have corrected all her faults; but I cannot persuade her to read, though she has an understanding memory and taste that would bear great improvement. But she is incorrigibly idle and lazy—thinks the world made for nothing but perpetual pleasure; and the deity she most adores is Morpheus."

Some weeks later, Miss Vanhomrigh complains that Swift does not answer her letters. But in what terms? By what means did the young ladies of that epoch—even were they " incorrigibly idle and lazy "—acquire so notable a style? " You must needs be extremely happy where you are, to forget your absent friends; and I believe you have formed a new system, and think there is no more of this world, passing your sensible horizon. If this be your notion I must excuse you; if not, you can plead no other excuse; and if it be so, I must reckon myself of another world; but I shall have much ado to be persuaded till you send me some convincing arguments of it."

Nearly a year later she writes: " I have been studying Rochefoucauld to see if he describes as much self-love as I found in myself a Sunday, and I find he falls very short of it."

And when Vanessa feels inclined to discourse upon politics: "How much we differ from the ancients, who used to sacrifice everything for the good of their commonwealth; but now our greatest men will at any time give up their country out of a pique, and that for nothing. 'Tis impossible to describe the rejoicings that are amongst the Whigs since that day, and I fear the elections will add to them. Lord Treasurer has been extremely to blame," etc. How many young women of to-day could frame so imposing a criticism for the benefit of a political friend?—although it is true that Vanessa—probably at a guess—sets "the ancients" a little higher than, perhaps, is strictly justified by the witness of history.

A year later, while in Berkshire, where he is staying with a friend, Swift writes: "I shall be glad to hear from you, not as you are a Londoner, but a friend. For I care not threepence for news, nor have heard one syllable since I am here."

Shortly afterwards occurred a break in the correspondence of about five years; and when it was resumed, Swift writes: "If you write as you do, I shall come the seldomer, on purpose to be pleased with your letters, which I never look into without wondering how a Brat, who cannot read, can possibly write so well."

The Dean might have reflected that Vanessa was his devoted pupil, and that her affection for him made her an apt student. For much has been written concerning the relations between these two stormy, passionate, and generous souls. It is no business of ours. The letters should have been destroyed. A box of old letters is sometimes as dangerous as a case of gunpowder. That Esther Vanhomrigh was fervently attached to the kind, witty, elderly friend who petted and spoiled the charming girl, was natural enough. None knew better than Swift the dangers of such a relationship. He tried to avoid them. The end of the story is sad enough. Mr Freeman tells all that it is necessary to know. Others have been less reticent. And the question is : By what right do strangers pry into these affairs, and constitute themselves judges of the dead? Is there no honour among men of letters, that they should purvey scandal under the guise of what they choose to call literary criticism, and use a brother who is dumb and defenceless, as they would not dare to use him were he alive, with his weapons to his hand? It is pleasant to think that their retribution is but postponed; that one of these days the terrible Dean—who, be sure, has long since made up his quarrel with Vanessa—will take them aside into a quiet corner, and read them a little homily.

MR PUNCH

IN 1921, at the Little Theatre, Adelphi, appeared a strange and an attractive presentation of the early history of Mr Punch, whose tragicomedy has been constantly performed for at least three hundred years, and, for aught we know, a thousand. Mr Russell Thorndike, who played Punch with an admirable skill, Miss Sybil Thorndike, who played Judy with an extraordinary feeling for the right grotesque, and their company, present what is none the less fascinating a story, because it is partly hypothetical. Mr Punch, or Punchinello, came to England from Italy; and at the Little Theatre one beheld in a fantastic and a fitting Italian setting, a version of what may be the original legend.

Here Mr Punch, an important citizen, is presented with the Big Stick by the Mayor as a tribute to Mr Punch's civic virtues; whereupon Mr Punch is seized with an inordinate ambition for greatness. Now that he wields the Big Stick, Mr Punch will achieve with that weapon supreme power. He is warned by the Blind Man, a boding figure of whom alone Mr Punch stands in awe, that no good can come of the business; but Mr Punch will not take his advice. He makes away with everybody: with the Baby, the Doctor, the Mayor, the Beadle, the Hangman, Judy and the

Serving-maid—all, except the Blind Man; and he hangs their bodies over a rail in his garden, like washing. This formidable Mr Punch, clad in red-striped tunic and breeches, with his huge nose, fierce eyes, and high voice, becomes like some implacable avenging demon of a dream.

At the summit of his achievement, when he bestrides the dim stage in the moonlight, hugging his Big Stick, there comes to him the Blind Man, with his Dog, to deride Mr Punch and to pronounce his doom. What is it? It is that Mr Punch is so far from having attained a tremendous reputation, as he vainly imagines, that he is condemned to go down the ages as a figure of ridicule. Throughout the generations all the children in the street shall point fingers and fall into laughter at the man who thought he could achieve power by wicked violence.

You may say that here is a moral, and indeed it is an excellent moral. The play of Mr Punch at the Little Theatre is in fact a Morality play; and as the showman said at the beginning—though his wife would not agree with him—there is a meaning in the puppet-show given on the beach at the frivolous seaside, which people do not understand.

As for the relation of the play to the real origin of Mr Punch, it is of no great importance; for the simple reason that no one knows exactly in what the origin consisted. Some among the learned hold that the play itself is descended from the ancient pieces of the Atellanæ, and that Mr Punch was originally Maccus, the clown. In that case, Punch was a member of the troupe of Arlecchino and Brighella, or as we say, Harlequin and Columbine. Now it is said that Harlequin was himself descended from a Roman mythological play in which the god Mercury came to earth to rescue Psyche, who became Columbine. Hence, it is conjectured, came the spangles of Harlequin's attire, which represented the celestial radiance of the god, shining through his clothing; hence, also, his mask, which he donned to veil the intolerable brightness of his countenance.

But other learned men reject the theory. They derive the name of Punchinello from one Puccio d'Aniello, a landowner of Averra near Naples, who was gifted with the talent of the comic actor. Other scholars, again, conjecture that the first Punchinello, or Pulcinella, was one Silvio Fiorillo, whose part was improved by another, Andrea Calcese, surnamed Ciuccio. It is almost certain that the original Punchinello had something to do with a tavern, and that, being endowed with singular ability to play the clown, he joined an itinerant troupe of Italian mummers. He had a falsetto voice; hence the pan-pipes of the showman of to-day, and a great nose—which the puppet inherits.

The hunchback seems to have originated in France, in which a person so afflicted was customarily employed as a professional jester. It may be that it was not the deformity which amused, but the quaint humour with which—perhaps as compensation—the sufferer is gifted.

157

The first really authentic Mr Punch appears
at the Court of Louis XIV, in a puppet-play introduced by the Italian troupe of actors entertained
by that monarch. Mr Punch, upon his appearance
in France in the seventeenth century, was known
as Polichinelle, and to-day he is called Guignol.
From France, Polichinelle voyaged to England,
where he became a tradition as Mr Punch. He
may have come over with the Huguenots, or he
may have accompanied that saturnine monarch
William of Orange. In any case, both Pepys and
Evelyn refer to Mr Punch, in mentioning the
Italian puppet-show in Covent Garden.

As for Toby, nobody seems to know when or
how the little dog appeared. Perhaps Mr Punch
stole him from the Blind Man. It would be like
him. But when we have explored so far into the
past of the strange, beaked figure, high-voiced
and farcically cruel, haunting the memories of
childhood, we find traces of an older and a more
momentous play, in which Pulcinella contended
against Want and Weariness, as well as quarrelling
with his wife, defeating the police, and cheating
the Inquisition. This earlier and more imposing
Mr Punch was acquainted with the Patriarchs, and
was the familiar friend of the Seven Champions
of Christendom. So, by the dim light of the anti-
quary's lantern, Mr Punch flits among the shadows
of the forgotten centuries.

But whatever his strange parentage, Mr Punch
as we know him remains; and as we know the
play, it is an embodiment of that rough-and-

tumble humour beloved of our ancestors, the apotheosis of that venerable jest which consists in knocking a man down. One might go further, and hazard a guess that Mr Punch represents that jolly fancy most of us have entertained, the picture of how satisfying it would be if we could suddenly remove every one whom we disliked. It is the tempting illusion, indeed, of absolute power; for the surrender to which temptation, as Mr Russell Thorndike showed, Mr Punch is doomed to endure the ridicule of the children of succeeding generations.

THE ANCESTRY OF SKELT

ふ

THE essay *A Penny Plain, Twopence Coloured*, by Robert Louis Stevenson, has become a part of English literature. Who that reads Stevenson knows it not? Many, perhaps, to-day have wondered what exactly were those works of a peculiar art which so enchanted little Louis Stevenson in his rather austerely governed childhood. These pictures may still be purchased by the curious. They are crudely drawn outlines, sometimes garishly coloured, of figures, landscapes, and interiors. The original Skelt, to whom Stevenson traces their invention, designed these fantasies to make a kind of children's pictorial theatre. The idea was to cut out the figures and scenes, presumably to paste them upon cardboard or stiff paper, and with them to fit up a toy theatre with wings, back cloth, set scene, box scene, front cloth, and all the rest of it. Some children, doubtless, took a pleasure in this ingenious labour; but it is to be supposed that the most of them, like the young Stevenson, found their chief pleasure in colouring the 'plain' outline drawings, and in musing upon the admirable titles suggesting the plays they represented. Where are the plays? Evidently they were sold separately, for Stevenson refers to the "play-book," and no doubt some plays are still extant.

Stevenson justly observes that the pictures were all designed either for melodrama or for pantomime. He regards *Skelt's Juvenile Drama* as the transcription for the young of " the great age of melodrama . . . the kingdom of Transpontus," as of course it was; and he leaves it at that. Pantomime is another matter, which Stevenson puts aside.

But this singular incarnation of the art of the theatre, its reduction, so to speak, to its lowest terms, is significant of much which Stevenson left unsaid. He had no great notion of the theatre. He once remarked to a friend that the novelist had no need of the aid of an actor to interpret the novelist's characters to his audience; a remark which implies a certain misconception of the purpose of the theatre. There is a point at which the art of the novelist and the art of the playwright meet; but for the rest, their methods are essentially divergent. We are here dealing with melodrama, a word usually employed to signify a form of art whose effects are violent and unreal.

But these are relative expressions. They denote the opinion of that part of the public whose intelligence, being offended by melodramatic presentment, avoids these entertainments. But upon the audience which frequents melodrama its effect is neither violent nor unreal. So far from being offended, these happy people are enraptured. Stevenson speaks " of the footlight glamour, the ready-made, bare-faced, transpontine picturesque,

161

a thing not one with cold reality, but how much dearer to the mind!"

But here one must distinguish, for melodrama, dear to some, repels others. It appeals, in fact, to those who see life in those broad, fantastic, and passionate terms; or to those who, like children, knowing no better, naturally accept the presentment. Stevenson, having put away childish things, yet remembered with pleasure that epoch of his being. He has no more use for Skelt, but he recalls that magician with gratitude.

Some clever person once said he cared not who made the laws of his country, if he were allowed to make its songs. If he thus nobly implied that upon occasion he could do both, his aspiration is none the less admirable. That aspiration has been the guiding star of generation after generation of a strange and lovable people, for hundreds of years. They are called gleemen, wandering minstrels, strolling players. They began to voyage throughout Europe when the Roman theatre disappeared. Their ancestry goes back far into the days before history began. They made the Sagas; in Greece they made the wonderful stories Homer wrought into perfect, and therefore enduring, shape. But so far as England is concerned, we may conveniently pick up their trail in the Mystery and Morality plays which they performed, and which they probably wrote; and thence we come upon them in the early Elizabethan romantic (not classical) drama. If John Webster's *Duchess of Malfi* be not melodramatic, what is? What but melodrama are the plays of Peele and Nash, Middleton, Ford, Beaumont and Fletcher, Kyd, even Marlowe, and even some plays of Shakespeare?

Side by side with these plangent and terrific spectacles are Ben Jonson's vigorous, scholarly comedies, and the purely classic masques and tragedies of Buckhurst and the rest. Thenceforward the two streams flow side by side, occasionally intermingling, yet always distinguishable: but whereas the melodramatic tradition has scarce changed in essentials for centuries, the politer and more intellectual art alters with every vicissitude of fashion, and is coloured by each succeeding phase of knowledge.

Such, in a word, is the vast and innominate ancestry of Skelt: and his latest avatar is the cinematograph. A penny plain (colour is lacking) is now endowed with movement. Of speech it is still deprived; and thus the noblest attribute of the whole art of the theatre is wanting. These swift shadow-shows go by in silence, enthralling and oppressive. Skelt, to do him justice, never dreamed of a theatre stricken dumb. He might be, and in fact was, vulgar; he was silly; he was anything you like; but at his best he touched romance; and when he designed his *Juvenile Drama* he conceived his paper puppet-show moving to the high voices and honest laughter of children.

As for Skelt's forerunners, the many companies of poor strolling players, what do they say to one another, as they gather invisible in the darkness of the cinema-house, and behold their tunable hearty muse grimacing, speechless? "The Public," methinks I hear them whisper, "always comes back to the Legit. They always have, bless them, and they always will."

A REDUCTION TO ABSURDITY

WHEN Mr George Moore published a play [1] concerning which, he said, he had "written just a comedy that pleased myself," he took care that but few readers should share his pleasure; for the book, sumptuously done with handmade paper and admirable typography, is "privately printed for subscribers only by . . ." And here follows a legend in the Erse, or Gaelic, character, which the present writer owns he cannot decipher.

An account of the play itself need not be attempted. A description would do it wrong, for its charm resides in its wit and in its excellent prose. Here are clear and vivid lines which an actor should delight in speaking; and which not every actor could fitly convey. But it is with the extremely entertaining preface we have to do for the moment. In that document, Mr Moore explains the theory of the art of the dramatist and of the actor. The Irish are perhaps the wittiest race on earth, and (despite all delusion to the contrary) they are as remorselessly logical as the French. They are never better pleased than when they are exposing that difference between theory and practice of which human life is compact; but when you ask them for a solution of the riddle,

[1] In February 1921.

they maintain an amiable silence. Mr Moore, like Mr Bernard Shaw, will pose you a dilemma with all the cleverness in life; and while you are toiling to resolve it, he disappears round the corner.

Mr Moore, for instance, argues that the elimination from the modern theatre of the soliloquy and of the aside, in the interests of what is called realism, or truth to life, has deprived the drama of two valuable devices, and that nothing has been put in their place. Shakespeare, says Mr Moore, used both soliloquy and aside; and to-day " there are always many about who can avoid soliloquies and asides. But to do this, and skilfully, does not carry the dramatist, so it would seem, any nearer to Shakespeare than he was before; an unpopular doctrine this is, almost a heresy, but I will dare to say that it is better to write *Hamlet* with soliloquies and asides than *Monsieur Alphonse* without." That is true enough; but the intelligent reader will perceive that the argument, like two parallel lines, may be produced to infinity.

So with regard to Mr Moore's remarks upon the number of exits and entrances in the modern piece, which he reckons at an average of eighty-four in three acts.

" Have you never, Lantern," says Mr Moore, addressing an hypothetical dramatic critic, " hand on your heart, experienced a feeling of exasperation when in the third act a man says that he will go . . . on the terrace? In that horrid moment we feel dramatic art to be more straitened and artificial than the ballade, the kyrielle, the rondeau, the rondel, the Sicilian octave, or the sestina. In its seventieth exit or entrance the modern comedy attains to the artificiality of the chant royal, and you will admit that this form has never produced a poem."

Here the argument is again that, in the attempt to achieve realism, the playwright merely succeeds in producing a high degree of artificiality. But concerning what he ought to do, Mr Moore maintains a bright reserve. And his quest for reality, says Mr Moore, brings the dramatist to another dead end ; for, perceiving that under the stress of emotion a man is commonly deprived of speech, the playwright reduces his actor, if not to silence, to as few and as inexpressive words as possible. The next stage in the process (though Mr Moore does not mention it) is the static play, as it is called, in which the characters neither move nor speak. And the final development is the play which is all scenery and no actors at all, concerning whose production Mr Gordon Craig has written a book, a serious work which, not unnaturally, is extremely antipathetic to actors.

These discussions are interesting, but they bewilder. There is in truth no way out on this level. Technical methods in themselves have no value. They are good or bad solely in proportion as they help or hinder the effect of the play as designed by the dramatist and interpreted by the actor. If the effect of a play be achieved, the means by which it is achieved are of no moment whatever. And whether or not the effect desired be accomplished depends first of all upon the comprehension by the dramatist, not of his public, but of the art of the actor.

Every artist works under conditions. The dramatist works under severely limited conditions of time and space. There is no mystery about these things. There "are always many about," as Mr George Moore would say, who can master them. But these are mechanical matters. The art of the actor is a living thing. Unlike all other artists, the actor's only instrument is himself. He alone, in his own person, bodies forth a work of art. The painter deals in pigments and canvas, the sculptor works in marble, the musician employs beautiful and complex instruments, the writer wields the most powerful influence in art, which is words. And what does the actor? In one way or another he uses all these arts, and to them he adds the peculiar gift of the mime, eloquent gesture. That incomparable vehicle of expression, the human body, is at the service of the dramatist. While the art of the dramatist and the art of the actor are not often exercised by the same person, they are in fact indissoluble. The words of the great French master remain. All he wanted was two actors, four boards, and a passion.

It is curious to remark how in most criticisms (such as the disquisition of Mr George Moore) the dramatist writes of his art without reference to the actor, while the actor disdains the playwright. It is even said that the dramatist is the true artist, and that the art of the player is merely mimetic, an imitation and not the real thing. Here is a strange confusion. It arises from the endeavour to treat as two things what is really one thing; from the habit, customary among critics, of regarding processes in detail rather than the effect of the whole, and from a misconception of the meaning of the word imitation. All art is imitation, but in the sense defined by Aristotle, which may be briefly paraphrased as development from nature to the ideal.

Nature is seldom perfect, yet man can conceive perfection, and it is the business of the artist to strive to attain it. There is no hierarchy among the arts. None is afore or after the other. Each is judged, not by its method, but by the degree in which the effect desired is achieved. To that end, all means are legitimate; but in practice some are found more useful than others. That is all. None knows it better than Mr George Moore; but then that ingenious artist, like other Irishmen, finds a pleasure in conjuring with words.

III : *THREE SKETCHES*

PORT OF LONDON

TO Londoners who dwell west of Aldgate Pump the river is nothing; it makes no part of their mental picture of London; unless perchance their Chelsea windows overlook the mirror of the sunset. When they think of the Thames, they think of Richmond, Henley, Shiplake, Mortlake, Sonning, and the rest of the bead-roll of pleasant names charged with happy memories. But upon the flood coiling beneath the London bridges burdened with impetuous tugs and drowsy barges, Londoners look askance. There are millions living within hearing of the steamers' sirens to whom it has never occurred to embark upon the river in a boat. They are dimly apprehensive of the powerful tide, sweeping up for five hours and down for seven, every day and night, with a twenty-foot fall and rise. Besides, nobody takes a boat. It is not done.

Nevertheless, it can be done. And once afloat upon the broad stream, you pass into another world which is not London though it is in the heart of London. On either hand, remote and silent, rise tall buildings and distant spires; but with the myriad crowded streets which lie over there, we have no more to do. We have passed to the lift and the breath of open water and the further sea.

We are made one, also, with that strange

brotherhood of the river which prevails from Teddington to the Nore; provided, that is, you know how to behave. There are rules to be observed. There is the Rule of the Road, which is international. There is the Rule of Courtesy, which allows plain language if the Rule of the Road is infringed. There is the Rule of Help. If you want a tow against the tide, you but have to sheer alongside a tug (if you can, for she will not stop), heave a rope and make fast. A trifling compliment in silver at the end is understood. Put a man across the river and he will pay you twopence, and refusal of the fare is not permitted. The vigilant, silent River Police, sliding by in a black motor-boat, are your friends. Having seen you once, they know you ever afterwards. If, drifting down through the Pool, with its steamers loading and unloading at the wharves, and its tugs bustling to and fro, and its massed flotilla of lighters: if then, a tug towing a long line of barges suddenly curves right across the stream ahead, you have but to obey the gesture of the tug captain and safety is assured.

And then you go down between the shores of a new city: a city of wharves, docks, warehouses, canals, cranes, steamers, masts, wooden houses tottering on piles, mud, and factories. That is the city east of Aldgate Pump; a city as unknown as Baghdad to the western city. It is grim and squalid, but it is Port of London, the port from which men and ships depart to every ocean, and to which they return from every quarter of the globe.

The life of the Port of London has been limned, as it has never before been limned, by Mr H. M. Tomlinson, in his book *London River*. You may get the material details of the place from the guide-books; you may get the look of it and the smell of it by simply going there—and the odds are you will return with a certain distaste—but the life you will never get save from one who has lived it, and who understands what he is living. Such an one is Mr Tomlinson. He has the faculty of perceiving beauty, and of expressing it beautifully.

One who has voyaged to that place by water and also by land; who has been nearly arrested for landing by chance on the foreshore of the Tower; who has been refused change for a sovereign because he wore a scarf instead of a collar; and who has even returned from these adventures with that indefinable distaste; can affirm that Mr Tomlinson is telling the truth. But Mr Tomlinson also knows that there is nothing to be afraid of; because he knows the people themselves. Above all, he knows the sailor; the merchant seaman who is scarce altered since Shakespeare met him somewhere down by Eastcheap, talked with the boatswain home from Prospero's Island, and then went back to his lodging and wrote *The Tempest*.

London to the sailor is but a port of call. He has, perhaps, a home there, and a wife, and still it is but an episode wedged between his voyages. You may say the place is unlovely and even villainous; but have you ever known what it was to

walk on firm ground amid the comfortable security
of crowds, after voyaging months upon the immense and inhospitable desolation of the sea?
" It is impossible," writes Mr Tomlinson, " for
those who know them to see those moody streets
of Dockland, indeterminate, for they follow the
river, which runs from Tooley Street by the
Hole-in-the-Wall to the Deptford docks, and
from Tower Hill along Wapping High Street,
Limehouse and the Isle of Dogs, as strangers
would see them. What could they be to strangers?
Mud, taverns, pawnshops, neglected and obscure
churches, and houses that might know nothing
but ill-fortune. So they are; but those ways hold
more than the visible shades. . . . But the call
comes again just where the stairs, like a shining
wedge of day, hold the black warehouses asunder,
and show the light of the river and a release to the
outer world. And there, moving swiftly across
the brightness, goes a steamer outward bound."
And again : " From my high window in central
Dockland, as from a watch tower, I look out over
a tumbled waste of roofs and chimneys, a volcanic
desert inhabited only by sparrows and pigeons.
Humanity burrows in swarms below the surface
of crags, but only faint cries tell me that the rocks
are caverned and inhabited, that life flows there
unseen through subterranean galleries." But " In
that distant line of warehouses is a break, and
there occasionally I see the masts and spars of a
tall ship, and I remember that beyond my dark
horizon of warehouses is the path down which

she has come from the Indies to Blackwall. I said we were not inland. . . . We are the hub whence all roads go to the circumference."

You catch the vision? "I said we were not inland." No more inland, indeed, than the sea-gulls which wheel and hover, uttering their harsh cries, about the Embankment, where the people feed them, and they catch the morsels in the air. Read, then, in Mr Tomlinson's smooth and beautiful prose, so delicate and humorous and restrained, *A Shipping Parish*, with its admirable picture of an interior, wrought with the skill of a Dutch masterpiece, and its fine figure of the old deep-water seaman. Read the story of the cobbler who set sail for the Spanish Main. Study the subtle sketch of *The Master*. Read *The Ship-runners*, a story even comparable with Mr Conrad's *The Heart of Darkness*. Consider *The Illusion*, with its wonderful mingling of past and present; and voyage, if you will, to the Dogger Bank in *Offshore*. Do not say, "Oh, only a collection of short stories," because you would be mistaken. *London River* is a great deal more than that. It is a work of art, coherently informed throughout with that rare essence which we recognize but for which we have no name.

WILD DAFFODILS

∽

THE train slackens speed as the miles
lengthen from the vast disarray of town
and suburb, and the sky lightens, and on
hiteer hand—the quiet fields lie among brown
hedges. From the wayside station, which is always
exactly the same, the gleaming rails run to the sea
beyond the hills; you have but to walk a few
steps, and the country receives you. The air blows
sweet and mellow, tinctured with a fragrance of
gorse in bloom. Here and there the hedgerows
are touched with green; the further woods, fret-
ting the broken sky, are faintly washed with
crimson; beside the field path cluster primroses,
and a patch of anemones glimmers white and new.
A bird sings sudden and clear and falls silent. On
the ridge of the ploughed field, whose surface is
caking into dust, stands a lonely plough, its handles
projecting like horns.

Spring comes in England like a wilful queen,
entering upon her kingdom determined to rule,
determined to give her subjects a taste of her
quality as she feels inclined, rather like the Queen
Elizabeth of the stories. To-day her Majesty
chooses to robe herself in azure embroidered
with sunlight. A brisk wind blows from the
west; the sky is laced with flying shapes of
clouds; beyond the rich meadows merging into

reddening woods, the strong-backed hills rise blue and clear.

This is a country of meadows of a noble amplitude, and oak thickets, and sudden, rounded eminences. Southward broods the long dim rampart of the Downs, taking the huge buffet of the westerly gales, keeping the wide and wooded valley in peace. The daffodils are shining in the garden, and a great bush of yellow flowers blooms against the weathered brick of the cottage. "It is one of the old-fashioned roses," says the old lady who has dwelt among the roses during fourscore years. "I don't rightly know the name." The pear-tree is dressed all in white blossom. Upon the intense rare blue of the sky are graven the glossy twigs of the old, twisted apple-tree, set with tiny and bright-hued buds.

As the sun falls to the west, garden and field and wood are bathed in a radiance of rose and gold, and the cows wander leisurely, yet with an air of slightly aggrieved dignity, past the shining pond (across which a moorhen flutters to her nest in the sedge) and along the grassy lane, and into the dusty white road, and so home. Beyond the darkling trees the fires of sunset burn with an orange glow. A light shines in the cottage window. Within, a great fire of logs flames and crackles in the wide ingle, ruddily touching the oak beams, and casting black shadows in the corners. Shut door and lattice and draw close about that comfortable blaze. There is no such thing in London.

Without, the wind has gone down; the air is

chill; a great round moon hangs in the profound blue; and an immense silence enfolds the landscape. Early the next morning, a noise of tapping sounds in the silent house. What is it? There is no one at the door. Looking from the window, one beholds the sky white and clear, the fields glittering with frost and solitary, the garden all sparkling white and empty. Still the tapping. It is a goldfinch, perched on the ledge of the glazed panel in the door, tapping the glass with his beak. As the door is open, if he wished to enter, he could enter; but he is a perfect little gentleman. Presently he flies away and sits in the apple-tree, waiting for breakfast.

Another day of sun. The wood, from which they have cleared the undergrowth, is floored with red leaves and vivid moss, and bright primroses. A rabbit strolls from his cavern in the bank, and sits very still, and presently remembers an engagement and hastens away, with his rocking-horse gait, to keep it. All day the west wind blows steadily through the sunlight; and the head cowman says it is a day on which " you can lay down anywheres and be comfortable." But towards afternoon the sky is edged with little horizontal banks of·purple cloud; sure sign of a change of mood. The sunset peers angrily from under darkening brows.

The morning breaks with a cold and a bustling wind, moving continents of cloud, and flying gleams of sunlight. The face of the countryside takes on an aspect of a curious unshadowed clearness, tree and stile and cottage distinct and separable, the lichen on the wall vivid, the grass by the roadside individual, the cluster of primroses showing a brown edge to the petals. . . . Cold drops of rain fall; yet there is a sense of fair weather in the air; and towards evening the wind drops, and a faint sunlight comes and goes.

Across the pasture, and then round the field where the wheat is springing, and then across the fallow, and past the timbered, solitary farmhouse beside the thousand-years-old oak, there spreads the wide meadow in which grow the wild daffodils. Upon the green are laid as with a brush spaces of bluer green, where glimmer the gold flowers. A beam of sunlight strikes through the tangled coppice, casting long shadows across the grass, and touching the wild daffodils to brighter gold. Let us pluck them while we may, and carry them home, these beautiful ensigns of the beautiful wild wanton, spring.

OUT OF WORK (POST-WAR)

M R RICHARD JOBSON sat in an elbow-chair beside the window. He had been drinking a little, but not much. Men who are out of work drink that little because it blurs the edges of things.

Mrs Jobson was dabbling at the sink in the corner. Washing up occupied her for many hundreds of hours in the year.

"They sent for the piano this morning," said Mrs Jobson.

"Well, you never played on it, that's one comfort," said Mr Jobson, elliptically.

"No. I never wore me fur coat, neither. Nor I don't intend to wear it." Mrs Jobson spoke as one conscious of merit. "But I suppose it will have to go."

"You keep your fur coat, old dear," returned her husband, placidly. "There's several little things can go first. No objec' in getting excited because you're out of work. 'Taint the first time, M'ria."

"But it's the first time we 'ave paid these prices, Rich. How we're to live, I don't know. If you was to go and do a bit of shopping like I do, Rich, you'd understand."

"It's never been very different, as I see," observed Mr Jobson. "Except in the War."

" It's gone, any'ow," said Mrs Jobson. " I had a feeling at the time it couldn't last for ever."

" No one but a fool thought it *would* last for ever. All this here talk about a New World—I heard it all before. It don't mean nothing. So long as a man gets his money coming in regular, the old world's good enough for me. We was better off with the low wages and the cheap prices."

" What about no wages at all, Rich? "

" Well, what about it? There'll be a job along, presently, for a man who ain't afraid of work. All these young fellers, they've got what they call the New Spirit. Take all they can get and give nothing for it. I'm all for a bit of the New Spirit myself, in moderation. But these boys they overdo it, and then they find themselves among the ruddy unemployed. The New Spirit ain't so new as they think. I seen it before they was born. Always ends the same way. In the street, or else the work'us."

Mrs Jobson, drying her hands, glanced towards the two silver-framed photographs standing side by side on the mantelpiece. One represented a sergeant, the other a corporal.

" I can't help but think, God forgive me, them that's gone is the lucky ones," said Mrs Jobson. " There don't seem much left, do there? " She sat down in the worn chair beside the smouldering fire, her face gone suddenly old. " I don't see what us can do," she said.

Mr Jobson regarded her gravely. The red

beam of the sun, striking from beneath the edge of a rain cloud, lit the portraits of the two soldiers.

"See it through, I reckon, same as Bert and Alf did," said Mr Jobson, his gaze shifting for a moment to the photographs. "They was never beat. And I'm not beat. And you're not beat, neither."

"I believe you're right, Rich." Mrs Jobson, strong and square, rose sturdily to her feet and began to set the tea-things. Mr Jobson watched her with approval.

"That's the old spirit, that is, Mother," said Mr Jobson. "You can't better it. I took partic'lar notice of this here war, and all what's happened since, while the others was talking, and I reckon the old country is on top of the world, when all's said and done."

"You've had half a pint and see things rosy-like," said Mrs Jobson. "Suppose you're mistaken?"

"Won't make no difference," said Mr Jobson.

He sat silent and massive beside the darkening window, while his wife lighted the lamp.

IV : *THE FIRST ANNIVERSARY*

FOR REMEMBRANCE

A T eleven o'clock on the forenoon of Thursday, November 11, 1920, a hush fell upon
city and town and village. The King stood
in Whitehall, over against the flag-draped coffin
of the nameless fighting man; hard by stood
his Admirals of the Fleet, Field-Marshals and
dignitaries; on either hand were ranked his sailors
and soldiers; and behind them stood the silent
multitudes. At that moment, the wheels stopped,
and men and women stood motionless; the
foot-passenger, the worker beside his machine,
the labourer beside his plough. The whole immense drift of life and thought was halted, and
uplifted into another region; and in that silence,
the dust and the conflict and the pleasure forgotten, all men were as one; for all stood in the
presence of that which makes all men equal.

They emerge from that interval not quite the
same, perhaps, as they entered it. Not ours to
read the minds of men; yet we may say, as it
was said of old, upon a like occasion, " It is good
for us to be here." Many of us, at least, recalled
in those moments the unique and shining remem-
brance of the spirit which filled the whole air of
the fighting-zone, and which it is impossible to
convey in words. The effect was of a quick and
new life (as of another planet); of the superb

reign of ordered power; and, strange as it seemed at home, of a release from all anxiety.

And a part of the cause was the consciousness of the single purpose and the combined and eager obedience to it of a great host of men who trusted their leaders and one another. It seems sad that it needs a frightful war to create, or, to be more precise, to awaken, that spirit; that we have still to recapture it in peace. But at least we have looked upon its brightness, and that is good for the soul; and it is right that every year the nation should thus return in unison to the things that belong unto its peace. Never did his Majesty the King more nobly exercise his high office than when he called his people to the Silence. Indeed, it may be that there could be no more salutary exercise for the nation than the daily practice of the annual public ceremony. It is said by the philosophers that the victory of the War was the victory of the spiritual element over its material antagonist. If that saying be true, then it is also true that the warfare is eternal, and that when armies take the field, it is but the same warfare translated into terms of shot and steel.

There was one effect of the tremendous ceremonial which perhaps was not foreseen, and which perhaps can only be rightly apprehended by those who witnessed it. For these noble obsequies, celebrated with all regal magnificence in the sight of thousands, brought again to the hearts of the bereaved the first shock of the thrust which pierced them during the War. Their hidden

trouble was, as it were, lifted into the sunlight
to receive the tribute of the great ones of the
earth ; and, though it was thereby exalted, it was
an exaltation wrought with a sharpness of pain.
Every one of those who suffered loss, who beheld
the King saluting the fallen, and whose heart-
strings were riven by the terrible roll of the
muffled drums, must have entertained the strange
new thought of the immense and the supreme
value of the life consummated upon some dark
field of battle or whelmed in the deep sea. But,
if the sense of loss was thus sharpened, how as-
suaging the consolation that all, with one accord,
from King to day-labourer, pay to it their noblest
homage. It is a bitter thing to bring a gift, the
dearest in life, and to find it lightly taken. There
can be no such reproach any more.

There is, in fact, no parallel in history for the
celebration. Alike in Paris and in London, the
day must be marked as significant of what may
be a new era in the world ; not the fruition of
the delirious schemes for the rebuilding of this
scarred and weary old arena of the gladiator
Man, but something in default of which his every
conflict ends in defeat.

The splendid and triumphing strains of the
Funeral March have rung to their majestic close,
the Last Post has sounded ; the dust of France is
sprinkled above the mortal remains of the dead
fighting man who sleeps now in the Abbey ; and
the wheels of life are set grinding again. If,
indeed, we are fated to continue in the old way

of internecine strife and the fight for a living, climbing upon one another's shoulders, and let who will be pressed down into the mud; if so, we say, let us nevertheless take heart of grace and do what the fighting men did, which was simply to go cheerfully straight ahead with the next job. They came through, and not a single private soldier but did a deal more, slogging along in his humble way, than ever he knew or dreamed. For the Cenotaph stands to remind us, not only of a high achievement, but of a great example, to hearten and to inspire.

A YEAR AFTER

A YEAR passes, and again the nation pays its homage to the living and the dead, saluting in silence the men and women who fought and toiled in the Great War, both those who are still with us and those who have put off the vesture of mortality and have put on immortality. In the hush and pause so wisely decreed, we may all of us step aside from the deceptive appearances of life, and dwell for a moment with the unseen and the eternal. Strife, it seems, is a condition of our being; all things are born of conflict; for all that we hold dear we must still contend; nevertheless, it is possible to look beyond the dust and turmoil, and to perceive (if only for an instant) the essential unity of man. It remains to be achieved; and albeit by the war of diversities, it must yet be accomplished.

In the memory of the brave gift of life and all its promise, all are at one; the steadfast and the erring, the froward and the wise, alike. Quarrels and cares and ambitions, fears and hopes and sorrow, fall away and dwindle to their true proportion beside a single tremendous and shining verity.

There are very many who stand upon the threshold of the unseen and scrutinize the darkness beyond. If they perceive no glimmer in the void, then their lot is hard indeed. For if those whom they have lost are lost for ever, then we who remain can but linger out our tedious days to the dull close which extinguishes sensation. But to the massed thousands who last year beheld the obsequies of the unknown Warrior, it was impossible to attribute the sorrow of those who are without hope. In so far as their thought might be divined, in so far as their mind might be interpreted from those miles of still, grave faces, they felt all about them a presence unseen. Was it wholly fantasy that the bright haze of the autumn morning was not all empty air? There were women weeping; but ere the high strain of music fell fainter in the coloured distance, the look in their eyes seemed to image more than hope. It was as if with their inner vision they beheld a sign.

THE FACE AT THE WINDOW

THE three women seated at the upper window, which directly overlooked the Cenotaph, were dressed in mourning, and they stared upon the tall monument bearing upon its side the three flags, whose golden staves were planted upright upon the honey-coloured stone: the ensigns of Navy, Army, and Mercantile Marine. The yellow roadway, closed in on either side with banks of silent people, stretched away into the mist. Silent people filled the windows of the sombre buildings opposite, the sills of which were draped with squares of purple. Above the roofs, the flags drooped half-mast upon the lucent sky.

The woman in the centre of the group of three was weeping. Which among the three flags fastened upon the Cenotaph covered the man she had lost? The faces of the women on either side of her who was weeping were set and pale. They looked and looked at that strange spectacle, the strangest England has ever seen.

And now there stole upon the senses an unforeseen effect of this noble and honourable pageant. We had thought our trouble was secret, buried in the mind, hid from the light of day and tended like flowers upon a grave; when, behold, what we thought was our private grief is suddenly

blazoned to the sunlight and the multitude by
all the Kings, Princes, Dignitaries and Powers
majestically assembled. This, then—*this* for the
lad who fell out there in the roar of battle. . . .
It is as much as a person can endure. So the
woman at the window wept openly, and her friends
on either side held their faces set like marble.

There rose upon the still air the faint, far
wailing of the pipes, and then came the nearing,
magnificent music of the Funeral March, tearing
at the heart. There is a gold flash in the mist, and
the lion-hued firing-party, arms reversed, comes
pacing in front of the massed bands, while the
challenging music fills the air.

The woman at the window wept no more. Her
gaze was rapt above the pageant and the marching men and the flag-draped coffin borne on the
gleaming gun-carriage. She was gazing into the
curious grey mist thickening even then above
the procession, closing down upon the roofs, dim-
ming the sunlight. What did she behold, as the
music pealed, and the muffled drums thundered?
What was there in that curious grey mist?

Many years ago, a gifted lady wrote a wonderful book, and she called it *The Beleaguered City*.
She told how upon an ancient town in France
there descended a cold grey mist, thick and dark
and dry; and how in that darkness, by day and
night, the Dead returned to their old homes; and
how the living inhabitants fled from the city in
terror. But there was one who stayed, because he
was not afraid to greet the Dead who were not

dead. Surely he must have stared into the cold grey mist with the very look of the woman at the window, who gazed like one entranced into the haze which so remarkably brooded upon and followed the funeral train of the Soldier.

As the troops formed up south of the Cenotaph, while on its other side the King stood facing the gun-carriage, the grey mist paused and lifted a little in the profound silence. If there were thousands watching in the long street with caught breath, surely there were more thousands close about them, soundless, invisible, but felt. It is certain their presence was felt. It may be there were some who saw that the face of the woman who had been weeping was transfigured.

Nearly a million men obtained the Great Release, and many noble women. Their mortal bodies are mingled with the dust of desolate battle-fields, and on the deep sea floor their bones are strewn. Each and all left a memory of the last good-bye, of the torture of suspense, of the final stroke. To each among the hundreds of thousands of the bereaved, his or her particular agony. On Armistice Day, when the roll of the terrible muffled drums, and the rending bugles blowing the Last Post, wrench the secret from the heart's core, should those battalions of the Great Release not hear and understand? That is the question the preachers and the poets ask. Perchance they may know. Are they not perhaps alive? Do they not certainly dwell in our hearts, and is not that existence immortality enough?

No. It is not enough. Too long have we been put off with these timid questionings. And to-day there are those among us who know. When the great Funeral March breaks into its triumphing and victorious close, their hearts answer to it. Nearly a million men and many noble women, the flower of England, have passed the grave and gate of death, and they are stronger than Death. The Cenotaph is more than a memorial, more than the sad monument of broken lives. It is a meeting-place. Those who beheld the strange grey mist follow and brood upon the splendour of the funeral pageant, who felt all about them the stir of thronging, invisible life : should these need more assurance, they can obtain it.

As the last strains of the music died away in the massed tramp of marching men, and the base of the unveiled Cenotaph grew bright with high-piled flowers, the faces of the three women at the window changed to a look of peace.

IN THE TWILIGHT

～

"SO that's over," said the soldier. "Lights out. And very handsomely done, too. King George and all." His hand went to the salute and sharply down. "Some of us chaps would have smiled, if they'd been told it was to happen. They wouldn't have believed it."

The soldier contemplated the sculptured rock of the Cenotaph. Rising amid mounded blossoms in the twilight, it shone white and clean.

"I mind riding along here on the top of a bus, my first leaf," went on the soldier. "Wanted to know which was the Horse Guards, and the Admiralty and Nelson on his pillar. A civvy told me, same as it might have been you, sir."

"Very likely it was," I said. As I looked at the soldier, the later years departed, and I saw again the tawny, fierce-eyed men, hung about with accoutrements, nursing their rifles, staring at the dull turmoil and the sombre buildings; while I stared at the soldiers, for never before had Londoners beheld men like these men.

"I mind," continued the soldier, "coming on leaf that first time (but I never got another), and expecting to find the old country all a-stir and brisk and like electric in the air, same as in France. But it wasn't that, not to the naked eye, it wasn't. All

197

flat it seemed to us chaps, like the Gover'ment beer. I remember thinking that there beer the wickedest thing ! . . . I don't say I was actually glad to be back in the Line, but there's no doubt it was a relief to the mind. In the Army, you see, you know what you got to do and you do it, and the rest ain't your concern. And whatever happens it don't signify. And that's right."

In the shadow the misty gleam of the lamps touched the rugged figure here and there, glistening upon the fur about the shoulders, outlining the heavy pack, revealing the mud caked upon the great boots.

" I can talk to you, sir," went on the soldier in his curious, low voice, " as I can't to every one. I tell you, I saw a lot of things on the Ridge on the day I was hit—*but I never saw to-day*. I saw the whole plain, all black and yellow, going ever so far eastward into the mist, and Jerry's trenches a-winding across it like a dead serpent, and the flashes of the guns, and in amongst it I see myself coming home when it was all over, and the lamplight in the kitchen, and the missis, and bacon and eggs for supper, and a fire a man could get properly warm at. And all contrary-like there kept running in my mind some words I read once in a story-book : *Them that die'll be the lucky ones*. But I never saw no picture of to-day. Never dreamed of it."

" You were in the procession ? "

" Ah," said the soldier, " I was there. In my official capacity, you'll understand."

I could understand that. But I did not understand why he laughed to himself.

"To see all the people," said the soldier, "a man would surely think all the fighting men were dead for ever, and all the people left alive would be alive for ever. It's really surprising to a man what knows the war is only civil life speeded up intensive, as it were. Coming and going all the time, that's what it is, and in the firing-line the difference between dead and alive isn't hardly noticeable. Owing to the speed of events, as you may say, and what you may term the atmosp'ere. Here, you'd think that people were certain sure they could set about making a new world all by themselves, and finish it."

"You mean that among the people who are left alive, trying to make a better world (as they say), many drop out and die, every day, so that they never see the end of their labours. Is that it?"

"Ah," said the soldier, "that's what it amounts to, in any big push, for a better world or what not, that's what it always comes to. Why, among the thousands what salute the dead to-day, there's some will join that company before revally to-morrow. There isn't a moment—not a single moment—when you can fall in all living persons on one side of a tape line, for surely they're crossing over as you look. But it's more than that. If you want a big job done, *you mustn't lay down that there tape*. That, I reckon, was what they tried to do to-day. Leave all the dead men where they lie, put down the tape, toe the line, and start again at zero."

"But you would not have the nation fail to honour the men who——"

"No, no," said the soldier. "That's kindly. That's right. The men what's gone, they don't forget, neither. No. All I say is, don't put them away, out of your thoughts. You was speaking of making a push for a better world. You—the Living, I mean—can't do it by yourselves, you know. I ask you, sir, has it ever been done yet?"

In the light of a transient vision of dead cities, and fallen temples, and the savage squalor of London festering about us, clearly the answer was No.

The soldier turned away, facing towards the carved stone cliff of the Abbey, towering upon the dim violet of the dusk.

"In there," said the soldier, "they read a piece out of a book about the Communion of Saints. But they don't seem to take much notice of it, by what I can see."

"Perhaps it was in their minds when they buried the Unknown Soldier there," I said.

"Ah," said the soldier, in his singular, inward tones, "the Unknown Soldier. Unknown? He's not unknown among the Dead."

For the first time he turned his face to me. In the hazy shaft of lamplight, the broken peak of his cap threw so black and jagged a shadow that it was as if there was a hole in his forehead. It was the shocking impression of a moment; the next, saluting, he had turned towards the Abbey, and his form was lost among the woven shadows and the drifting figures of the foot-passengers.

V : THE NAVY TRIUMPHANT

THE PIRATE FLAG COMES DOWN

⁓

DOWN in the wireless cabins during the
night of November 20-21, 1918, the boys
helmeted with the earpieces heard the German ships chattering to one another continuously,
talking in code. Then came a W/T signal from
the British Commander-in-Chief, ordering silence
to be kept in the German ships; and silent they
were and so remained. A breeze rose softly in
the dark and blew away the fog which had hung
over the Firth for a week, and the innumerable
ships' lights shone near and far. The Fleet was
to get under way at four o'clock on the morning
of Thursday the 21st. The evening before, it was
announced that breakfast would be at a quarter to
seven. That announcement, and the succession of
signals recording the exchange of communications
between the British and the German authorities,
posted in the ward-room, were the only symptoms
of the situation; nor did anyone discuss it. The
surrender for internment of the German vessels
had become merely the evolution of the day, an
interruption of harbour routine.

To the writer, a guest on board H.M.S. *Hercules*,
it was as if the war had never been : as if four years
had dropped out of life, and he woke to find himself once more at home in the Navy, savouring the

peculiar atmosphere of the still, bright-lit 'tween decks, the throbbing of the dynamos in his ears; hearing the bugles call and the ships' bells striking, close at hand and distant; surrounded by the same placid, ordered energy, exact and unhurried and inevitable; hearkening to the histories of old shipmates, lost to all knowledge during the four years' void; pacing the wet, honey-coloured deck in the shrewd salt air, and marking, with the old bewilderment, the singular contrast between the vast array of ships and the ignorance of them of the people on shore. . . . It is the same Navy; but in ten years, and especially in the last four of them, the ships have subtly changed and formidably grown. The change is as significant, the growth as palpable, as the development of the light-riding esquire into the mailed and panoplied knight-at-arms.

In the twilight of the dawn a spectral battleship hove toweringly astern as the squadron turned, and behind that visored giant glimmered another and another, vanishing back into the dark. The whole Fleet was proceeding to sea, towards a dull bar of orange rifting the sullen sky, and it was very cold. The writer, descending to breakfast, asked his neighbour if this was a "good-morning" ship; it is a point to be ascertained. "Sometimes," said the officer darkly. People who have been on watch for four hours do not crave for conversation but for food. And there were white bread, real butter, real jam, sugar, tea copious, unknown on shore.

On the bridge the Admiral and the Captain paced up and down; the Signals Officer, muffled in a thick, hooded jacket, with glasses slung about his neck, was continuously busy; the Navigating Commander pervaded the shelter projecting forward from the bridge, in which there was no helmsman. He was in the conning-tower below. Not until the War was the quartermaster eliminated from the bridge, on which there are now perhaps a dozen officers, including two midshipmen. On this occasion there were also Admiral Lorenzi and his A.D.C. representing the Italian Navy, in the trim black uniform of that service. The North Sea haze thickened upon the bright water some two or three miles away on either hand, and now and again a gleam of sun turned the ships suddenly white and blue-shadowed.

The Main Fleet was proceeding in two lines, each hidden from the other in the mist. The northern line, in which was the *Queen Elizabeth*, flagship of the Commander-in-Chief, Admiral Sir David Beatty, was led by the Fifth Battle Squadron, Vice-Admiral Arthur C. Leveson, flying his flag in the *Barham*. (In the *Barham* is the portrait of Lord Barham, First Lord of the Admiralty at the time of Trafalgar, presented to the ship by the late Admiral of the Fleet Sir Gerard Noel, and by his instructions fitted with plate glass and screwed to the bulkhead, so that it should remain in its place in action. And in action Lord Barham has remained, unhurt.) Then came the Sixth Battle Squadron (United States Navy), Rear-Admiral

Hugh Rodman, U.S.S. *New York*; the Second Battle Squadron, Vice-Admiral Sir John M. de Robeck, *King George V*; and the First Battle-Cruiser Squadron, Rear-Admiral Sir Henry F. Oliver, *Repulse*.

Ahead of the southern line were *Furious*, Rear-Admiral Sir Richard F. Phillimore, Flying Squadron, *Vindictive*, Captain H. E. Grace, successor to the *Vindictive* of Zeebrugge and Ostend, and *Minotaur*, Rear-Admiral Edward F. Bruen, Second Cruiser Squadron.

The southern line of the Main Fleet was led by the Fourth Battle Squadron, Vice-Admiral Sir Montague E. Browning, flying his flag in *Hercules*, Captain Lowndes. Then came the Second Battle-Cruiser Squadron, Rear-Admiral Sir Lionel Halsey, *Australia*.

The destroyer flotillas, numbering over a hundred vessels, Commodore (F) Grand Fleet Flotillas, Commodore Hugh J. Tweedie, flying his broad pennant in *Castor*, had gone ahead to meet the German destroyers, which brought up the rear of the German Fleet; and following the flotillas, also ahead of the Main Fleet, were the Light Cruiser Squadrons.

Preceding the northern line of the Main Fleet were the First Light Cruiser Squadron, Rear-Admiral Walter H. Cowan, flying his flag in *Caledon*; the Sixth Light Cruiser Squadron, Rear-Admiral Edwyn S. Alexander-Sinclair, *Cardiff*, Captain Claude H. Sinclair; and accompanying the northern line was the Fourth Light Cruiser

Squadron Rear-Admiral Allen F. Everett. Vice-Admiral Trevelyan W. Napier, Light Cruiser Force, was present, flying his flag in *Courageous*. Vice-Admiral Sir William C. Pakenham, Battle-Cruiser Force, flying his flag in *Lion*, took station astern of *Queen Elizabeth* in the northern line.

Preceding the southern line of the Main Fleet were the Third Light Cruiser Squadron, Rear-Admiral Allen T. Hunt, flying his flag in *Chatham* ; the Second Light Cruiser Squadron, Rear-Admiral James A. Fergusson, *Birmingham* (the first of his Majesty's ships to put down a German submarine) ; and accompanying the southern line was the Seventh Light Cruiser Squadron, Rear-Admiral George H. Borrett, *Cleopatra*.

The light cruisers *King Orry*, Commander E. Mosse ; *Blanche*, Captain Francis Buller ; *Boadicea*, Captain E. H. Edwards ; and *Blonde*, Captain Gregory C. Martin, proceeded between the lines, acting as repeating ships ; that is, to repeat the signals made by the flagships, so that the signals may be plainly seen by the whole line. With the Grand Fleet was the French armoured cruiser, *Amiral Aube*.

The Main Fleet and the cruisers numbered some seventy-six vessels ; the destroyer flotillas between one hundred and one hundred and fifty. This great array could not, of course, be viewed as one by any human eye, for even the observer in the balloon towed by the *Cardiff* could see only the ships within the moving circle of the mist. The *Cardiff* went ahead to meet the main German

Fleet at the rendezvous, "to direct the movements of the German main force and order them to proceed, if possible, at a speed of twelve knots."

The rendezvous was fifty miles out at sea, due east from the Firth. The general arrangement was that the British destroyers should there meet the German destroyers and should turn with them; that the British light cruisers should meet the German light cruisers and turn with them; that the northern line of the British Main Fleet should meet the German main force and, turning, precede the Germans; while the southern line of the British Main Fleet should also turn west, proceeding parallel with the northern line for a certain distance, and should then turn east again and, turning west again, take up a position astern of the whole German force. Thus escorted, the Germans were to be brought to their anchorage off Inchkeith Island. These dispositions, carried exactly into execution, must be apprehended in the abstract. The spectator can see only what falls within his own field of vision.

At 7.50 on that Thursday morning the officers and men were all at action stations. Below, the visitor passes little knots of men, each man equipped with gas-mask, silently waiting; that is all. On the bridge the sea routine goes forward: the Admiral occasionally giving a quiet order, the Captain pacing up and down, the officers coming and going, the midshipmen standing by. Below, on the signal-bridge, the signalmen are incessantly hauling up flags and hauling them down again.

At a little after nine o'clock the observation balloon towed by the *Cardiff* became visible above the haze on the left hand. Then, at 9.25, from out the gold wall of the mist there shone horizontal bars of brighter gold; and there was the German Fleet. A group of officers hung on the port rail of the bridge, gazing through glasses. "Are their guns pointed inboard?" asked some one. "Inboard," said some one else.

Glasses made visible the faint purple silhouette of the grim upper works of the German battle-cruisers. It was possible to count five battle-cruisers: *Seydlitz, Moltke, Hindenburg, Derfflinger, Von der Tann*—the huge *Hindenburg* conspicuous. Astern came the nine German battleships—five *Kaisers*, three *Königs*, and the *Bayern*; then the seven light cruisers and minelayers; and then the forty-nine destroyers, one destroyer having tripped over a mine and gone down on the way. One battle-cruiser, one battleship, and one light cruiser were still to come.

As the pirate ships steamed slowly westwards they were shrouded, save for an occasional gleam, in the bronze and golden mist. For half an hour the southern line continued eastwards, passing the Germans on the reverse course, then turned west, the long line of castled ships, as they curved, towering into view, and proceeded parallel with the German Fleet. The routine on the bridge went silently forward: Admiral and Captain pacing up and down, officers coming and going, flags sliding up and down the signal-halyards. At eleven o'clock Sir David Beatty made a signal: "The German flag will be hauled down at sunset to-day (Thursday) and will not be hoisted again without permission." The German Admiral subsequently protested against the order, when he was tersely reminded by the British Commander-in-Chief that the Germans were in a British port and that a state of war still existed.

At a quarter to twelve, the southern line of the Main Fleet turned eastwards and passed the German light cruisers, still almost invisible, and the flotillas of British destroyers steaming on the left flank of the Germans, the nearer sea covered with the array of long low craft swimming easily along. The southern line of the Main Fleet then took station astern of the whole fleet and proceeded eastwards, and the Admiral went to lunch with his guests. About three o'clock the southern line passed the anchorage off Inchkeith Island, rising dark upon the coloured sky. The Germans were dimly visible, lying motionless beyond the outer ring of anchored British ships, their evil power broken at last. The southern line glided on towards harbour, while the *Queen Elizabeth*, increasing speed, passed the leading ships, and as she passed them, for the first time the silence was broken, and the faint sound of cheering came down the line.

Sunset burned beyond the sombre hills of the Firth as the *Hercules* drew near to the bridge. She passed the Sixth Battle Squadron, the ships of the United States, with their latticed masts and their

look, as compared with the British ships, of light-
ness, and the huge mastless hull of the *Argus*, the
aeroplane ship, painted like a model farm. An
aeroplane sprang from the deck of the *Furious*,
almost brushed the port rigging of the *Hercules*,
and soared over the ship ahead, as a swallow skims
a hedge. The flagship lay at anchor below the
bridge as the *Hercules* slowly passed her. Her
ship's company, looking dwarfed like toy figures,
was massed on her vast quarter-deck; and the
officers and men in the *Hercules* cheered the
Commander-in-Chief. Inside of a minute Sir
David Beatty signalled his thanks.

So to anchor, far up the Firth, in the fading
light of the day's end. Behind the day's silent
and stately pageant lay the irresistible unfolding
of a great purpose, which for nearly four years had
been coiling unseen about the pirates, and which
suddenly revealed them crushed in pieces. The
instrument of that purpose was the British Navy.
Every long watch, every straining chase, every
shot fired, every action fought, every tiny piece of
routine faithfully performed, the patience, vigilance, sagacity, and determination : each and all
had its due effect. The campaign at sea was one
long battle, with now and again an action as an
incident ; the prize of battle is victory, and there
can be no victory without battle. Again and again
the pirates tasted the hot and resolute quality
of the British fighting, and the day came when
they would not encounter it any more. " The
enemy," said Sir David Beatty in his message to

the Fleet," has given testimony to the prestige and efficiency of the Fleet without parallel in history, and it is to be remembered that this testimony has been accorded to us by those who were in the best position to judge."

These were not honourable foes : let that never be forgotten for a moment. Germany deliberately pitted herself against an antagonist whom she knew would not, under what provocation soever, depart by a hairbreadth from the code of honourable warfare, and who, therefore, in the German view, fought under a disadvantage, which Germany intended to push to the utmost. To that end, Germany kept her Main Fleet out of action solely in order to support her submarine campaign. The scope and power of that support are not generally understood. They consisted in protecting the exits and entrances of submarines within a sea area whose limits were the capacity of the German Main Fleet to steam out and back again without encountering the British Main Fleet. The German High Seas Fleet, by making it dangerous or impossible for British light craft closely to blockade the German and Belgian coasts, and to lay and to sweep mines, took a chief part in the practical submarine war. The man-eating tiger stayed in his lair, watching his bloodthirsty little cubs go out to seek their prey, knowing that within range of his spring they were safe.

Thus, in order to attain a decision by piratical commerce-destroying, which is a secondary operation of war, Germany deliberately chose to

avoid battle, and so she brought about her surrender without fighting. For she hazarded all on
winning. Did she fail to win decision, she lost
all. Honour had gone long ago; the Fleet must
follow. When her last chance consisted in fighting
a general action, Germany could not fight. *But
the British Fleet had been fighting all the time*. The
operations of minesweepers, destroyers, patrols,
airships, aeroplanes, cruisers, and the Main Fleet
were all one and interdependent; for the British
Main Fleet held the German Main Fleet so
that, beyond a limited area, it could not touch
the smaller craft which were exterminating the
submarines.

The German Navy, having chosen the way of
unmitigated evil, itself poisoned the very springs
of morality, so that in due time its demoraliza-
tion was complete. You cannot teach men to be
partly good and partly evil; it must be one or the
other. The virtues of courage, loyalty, and hardihood cannot, as a psychological fact, flourish in the
same soil as vice, cruelty, and falsehood. They
did indeed impose a disadvantage upon their op-
ponents, but in so doing they consummated their
own ruin.

Germany, having elected to dispute the mastery
with the British Navy, to achieve victory must
have fulfilled certain conditions. First of all she
must have bred a spirit of an equal rectitude;
then she must bring to the conflict forces of an
equal, or nearly equal, power and skill; then she
must have challenged battle instantly. And then,

so narrow was the numerical superiority of British heavy ships,[1] so strange are the chances of war, she might have won. But Germany, of three essential conditions, fulfilled only one. She had forces of nearly equal power and skill. Germany wrought her own degeneration of spirit, and did not understand that battle, and battle alone, can bring victory. It followed that every action of the British Fleet, from the destruction of a mine by a humble trawler to the tremendous shock of a Fleet action, brought Germany nearer to the inevitable catastrophe. In so far as the British Fleet was inactive it accomplished nothing. To do nothing is to achieve nothing. The politicians assert that if a Fleet merely exists it fulfils its purpose. Never was a more extraordinary delusion. The German Fleet, after merely existing, has ceased to exist as a fighting force, and they were the blows of the British Fleet which killed it. Nevertheless, according to Mr Churchill, "The view of the Admiralty is that the silent but irresistible Navy in the Forth and at Scapa caused the Germans to surrender, without placing our ships in danger." It was the same politician who wrote that "without a battle we have all the most victorious of battles could give us."

Admiral Sir Reginald Custance, who throughout the War has steadily set before his countrymen

---

[1] Note in this connection the assertions of certain politicians that they sufficiently increased the Fleet before the war, and compare the British with the German forces engaged in the Battle of Jutland.

the ancient and irrefutable principles of sea mastery, wrote in the columns of *The Times* as follows :

" Was there no shock of battle in the Heligoland Bight, off the Falkland Islands, on the Dogger Bank, in the Jutland battle, and in the innumerable actions between the light surface craft and the submarines? Each of these actions had its effect on the armed strength of the German Navy in *matériel* and *moral*. Any lapse of time between them does not affect the principle that each fight at sea during the War may be looked upon as part of one great battle at sea. Their collective effect, coupled with the firm determination of the British and Allied Navies from admirals to skippers to attack whenever opportunity offered, brought about the mutiny of the German Navy, which saw itself threatened with destruction if it issued to fight. . . . The collapse of the German armed forces, whether on sea or on land, was brought about by the fight, or the threat of the fight, to which every other form of pressure was secondary."

To which one would add the incomparable exploits of the storming of Zeebrugge and Ostend, which signalized the return of the authorities to the true principle of British naval warfare.

We are here dealing, not with a question of opinion, but with a question of fact. The politician, distorting the fact, both insults the Navy and contradicts the teaching of a thousand years of sea warfare. It follows that the British people must judge the truth for themselves. If they neglect what is, after all, no very recondite task, they will presently find the politicians once more engaged in gambling for votes with the maritime security of the British Empire.

The surrender of the German Fleet in the North Sea was followed by the surrender of the German, Turkish, and German-occupied Russian ships of war in the Black Sea, to the British squadron; the opening of the Dardanelles; and the access to Constantinople.

RETROSPECT

∽

NO one who understands what a naval action really is regretted a bloodless termination to the War at sea. It became a trial of endurance; and, as of old, the British Fleet stuck it out the longer. Some of us remember that hot July of 1914, when all the air was feverish with rumour, and the hard sunshine mocked at holiday-making; when the Fleet was mobilized for manœuvres, partly demobilized, and mobilized again for war. It was said at the time that the Fleet was kept in full commission after its return to port from manœuvres. That was not so. Orders to demobilize were issued, and some of the men were actually on their way home, when the orders were cancelled. Then the whole Fleet put to sea and disappeared.

The first sign of the War at sea evident to landward folk was the appearance of the Reserve men travelling to their destinations from all over the country. The present writer, called to London, beheld a little party of Reserve men, tanned, moustached, and dusty, waiting at the railway station. On the pile of their brown canvas kitbags a Reserve man lay asleep, exhausted with his march; and the civilians eyed him curiously and gravely.

The present writer happened to be sitting in a

newspaper office, late at night, when the news of the first naval casualty came in, recorded in the blotted purple lettering of the tape. H.M.S. *Amphion*, light cruiser, had gone down. She was pursuing the German minelayer, *Königin Luise*, and had struck a mine dropped by the flying German. In those days the news of a disaster was a shock. Afterwards, the tidings that a battleship had been torpedoed was scarce worth mentioning. The first news is unforgettable: the bright light and close air of the room; the murmur of traffic without; the entrance of the messenger with the torn-off slip; and a King's ship gone down, somewhere far out on the North Sea in the summer weather. . . .

Thus, all unknowing, we entered upon the dark and terrible years of the Great War. How little we knew! No one, it seems, except Admiral Sir Percy Scott and Sir Arthur Conan Doyle, thought of a submarine war upon commerce. The Germans had inexplicably neglected to send their light cruisers upon the trade routes before the declaration of war. They might have sent out forty or so, and so dealt this country a blow from which it would have been hard to recover. The unprotected trade routes were the chief danger. The Admiralty quietly took over vessels of the Mercantile Marine, armed them, manned them from the Royal Naval Reserve, and sent them to the trade routes. The Admiralty enlisted a vast fleet of trawlers and drifters from the fishing fleets and sent them minesweeping. At first these craft were unarmed, and always they were exposed to submarine attack. Private yachts were enlisted for the patrol service. The whole coastal area was divided into naval districts, and the fairway was swept of mines right round the British Isles. The Crystal Palace was turned into a training depot for the Royal Naval Volunteer Reserve. These things were not done in a moment. They were done with a steady concentration and by virtue of the incessant and thankless toil of hundreds of unnamed persons, naval and civilian. The whole business of making a New Navy was an improvization achieved during war.

And where was the old Regular Navy? At sea, and destitute of a properly equipped naval base; at sea, steaming by day and night without lights, in peril of submarine attack; at sea, ready for action; and so able to cover the transport to France of the old Regular Army.

The first mistake the Germans made was to neglect to send their cruisers commerce-destroying. The second mistake the Germans made was in not instantly challenging a general action with the British Grand Fleet. Had they been beaten, they would still have inflicted heavy loss upon the British; they would still have been supremely powerful on land; and, secure behind minefields, they could have repaired their losses. Had the Germans fought at once, they would have attacked ere the British had attained the extraordinary proficiency their four years' war training earned them. Turn the board round, and imagine the

German Fleet at sea: would the British Fleet have remained in harbour in 1914? Not for an hour.

It is not the time, nor is the present writer the person, to deal with the strategy of the War at sea. He can treat only of such aspects of the War as are discernible by the student. And it seems that the course of the War has proved the validity of the traditional doctrine that the decisive factor in naval war is either fear of battle, or battle itself. Germany lost the only general action she fought. Thereafter she refused battle. Then she lost all. For naval war is in essence the fight to control sea communications. The winner of that fight shuts the sea to the enemy and keeps it open for himself. Therefore can he move ships and troops as he will and obtain supplies from abroad, while the enemy can do none of these things.

Victory in battle, or the dread felt by the enemy of defeat in battle, gives control of the sea. If the Main Fleet of the enemy fights and is destroyed, there is an end of him. If he is afraid to come out, or stays in for other reasons, he loses control of sea communications almost as surely as though he had lost a battle. But in order to ensure that loss it is necessary that he should be blockaded. And that is exactly what the British Fleet did to the German Fleet for four years and three months.

The word blockade is commonly used in two senses. It is necessary to distinguish. During the

War the British Fleet maintained the blockade of the enemy in his ports. That is the military blockade. The maintenance of that blockade enabled the British Fleet (when it was allowed to do so by the Government) to conduct the commercial blockade of Germany, which was in fact the prevention of supplies from reaching Germany, or the siege of the enemy by water. Controlling the sea, the British Fleet can stop every merchant ship. The British patrol vessels order the enemy or neutral ships to stop, and send an officer on board to examine her papers and cargo. If the officer has reason to believe she is carrying contraband of war, or enemy goods, or goods destined for the enemy, he sends the ship into port. These proceedings are the exercise of what is legally known as the Right of Search. When the suspected vessel is in port, the Navy's duty is done. The rest of the proceedings is the business of the Prize Court, which administers the Law of Nations. Any interference by the Government with the Prize Court constitutes a violation alike of Municipal Law and the Law of Nations. The illegal release of ships and goods by the Government prolonged the War from six months or a year to four years and a half. Not until the United States, entering the War, forced the British Government to observe the law, were plentiful supplies sent from this country and from elsewhere cut off from the enemy. That unparalleled treachery was not the fault of the Navy, which sent supply ships into port, sometimes at the rate of a hundred a week, *whence they were released by order of the Government*.

At the same time the Navy secured the passage of troops, munitions, and supplies from all parts of the world. When war broke out the German China Squadron left Kiao-Chiao, and the *Emden* began her course of commerce-destroying. After Rear-Admiral Christopher G. F. M. Cradock had been sacrificed with his squadron off Coronel, on November 1, 1914, the heavy ships of the German squadron, commanded by Admiral von Spee, were sunk on December 8, 1914, by Vice-Admiral Sturdee, off the Falkland Islands. The light cruiser *Dresden*, escaping, was hunted until March 4, 1915, when she was sunk off Juan Fernandez by the British cruisers *Glasgow*, *Kent*, and *Orama*. The *Emden* was put down by H.M.S. *Sydney*, Captain Glossop, November 9, 1914. These and other losses of the enemy are matters of history. British cruisers, on every sea, were sailing and fighting month after month, chasing enemy cruisers and disguised enemy raiders; and, although the enemy inflicted a good deal of damage, in course of time he was abolished.

The first few months of the War taught the British people that the war upon commerce waged by a few wandering and hunted cruisers was very much more dangerous than they had been led to suppose. The official theory was that the difficulty of replenishing coal would restrict the range of the commerce-destroyer; but the Germans speedily solved that difficulty by capturing coal at sea. But during the first year of the War a new and most formidable danger arose. Germany, perceiving that the control of the sea had passed to the Power which, supreme and unchallenged, held the German Navy impotent, devised a new use of a new weapon ; pitched overboard all international law, the custom of the sea, and the usages of humanity ; and began to sink merchant vessels, belligerent and neutral alike, without warning.

The submarine campaign was planned completely to nullify the command of the sea exercised by the British Navy. And at one time it nearly succeeded. The immediate task of the Navy was to defeat an enemy it could not see. And the Navy was taken unawares. While the inventors were at work devising engines to destroy the submarine, the tale of ships lost rose to twenty, thirty, and forty a week. So far as the British public were concerned, it appeared as if the whole tremendous power of the Grand Fleet, except that it prevented invasion, was made useless. But the British public, continuing to trust the Navy, remained perfectly composed. And gradually the Navy began to defeat and to destroy the enemy it could not see. What the British perhaps did not clearly understand was that the perpetual vigilance of the Grand Fleet, preventing the German Main Fleet from extending its covering influence, or protective power, to the submarine campaign beyond a certain range, made the defeat of the submarine possible. Before the end of the War the Admiralty had in commission some two thousand small craft hunting the submarine, together with seaplanes and airships. It is probable that ere the German Government sued for peace the spirit of the submarine crews was nearly broken. There is a limit to the endurance of human nature.

It is to the eternal honour of the British Navy that not only did the Navy valiantly accomplish the warfare for which it had been trained and for which it was at least partly prepared, but that, suddenly confronted with a perfectly new kind of particularly deadly war, the Navy so dealt with it that the pirates were first foiled, then suffered the most frightful losses, and finally were in the way to be completely defeated when the whole infernal German machine itself capsized on the top of them.

When we came to the end of the War, suddenly and almost unawares—after so long travail and tribulation that the senses were dulled—even then, ere more than a little part of the whole splendid and tragic history was made known, we discerned something of the immense triumph of the Royal Navy, and perceived that from the beginning the Navy ensured victory, and that the Navy alone made victory possible.

It was held before the War that in the event of a European conflict the British Navy, with the small Regular Army, would decide the issue. In those days the fighting potency of the aeroplane and the submarine was not considered. Nor, except by the late Earl Roberts, V.C., and those who supported him, was the tremendous power of a whole nation in arms foreseen. And by a most unfortunate turn of destiny, the very Government which denied the necessity of fighting a great war on land, alleging that a powerful fleet would serve our need, not only neglected to provide a fleet fit for its gigantic task, but betrayed those maritime rights by virtue of which alone the Fleet performs its office.

But in spite of all these disabilities, it is still conceivable that had Great Britain fought at sea only, the British Navy would ultimately have decided the issue. We must assume that the Law of Nations concerning the sea would have been observed by the Government; that, accordingly, commercial blockade, the siege by water, would have been strictly and sternly enforced from the beginning; that no commodities of any kind sent by sea would have been allowed to pass into Germany; knowing as we do know that the political interference with the blockade prolonged the War for at least three years. What would have happened? France might have been defeated, and Germany might have occupied the Channel ports. Germany (in brief) might have created a German Middle Europe and made broad her road across the vanquished nations to the East. The process would take time, and at every step Germany would create an undying antagonism. But what would be happening outside the German reach during that time? All her colonies would have been lost; as indeed they have been lost. Not a German ship could have put to sea. Not a ton of supplies could have entered Germany from overseas. Her export and import trade would have been utterly destroyed. England, so long as their resistance endured, would have supplied her Allies with ships, munitions, and money. The whole of her resources being devoted to the sea, England might have controlled the Baltic and stopped the Scandinavian trade with Germany. Even if Germany won the war on land, how would she profit so long as the seas were closed to her? Commanding the sea and all oversea sources of supply, England could have continued the war if need be for twenty years. Not so Germany.

These are speculations; but they are perhaps worth some consideration; for, if the maritime supremacy of the British Navy was the first essential of national security before the War, and before the use of the submarine, what is it now? Because the submarine has altered the conditions of naval warfare, by so much the more is it essential that England maintain her maritime supremacy. To that supremacy, won by the incomparable skill, daring, endurance, and valour of the Navy, the Allies of Great Britain owe nothing less than victory. . We in this country owe to the Navy victory; and also, under the good providence of God, that safety and comfort, sufficiency of food and drink, and preservation from the devastation of the barbarian, which Great Britain, alone among the Allies, enjoyed throughout the Great War.

The high and austere tradition of the Royal Navy once more in the long history of England saved the country, saved Europe, and saved civilization. And it put the fear of God into the tribes of Germany. Of the same spirit was the old Regular Army, which, dying where it stood, bequeathed its spirit to the New Army; and their achievement is no less superb than the achievement of the Navy. Before the War, the two fighting Services lived by a lonely tradition, aloof from the rest of the nation, apart from the corruption of public life, and unacquainted with the chicanery of commerce. Seamen and soldiers were ill-paid and subjected to official extortions, to which, indeed, they are still subjected. Theirs was the fight, and theirs is the victory, and to them the praise. Not, of course, that the nation has remembered what else is due to them.

But as the Navy, like the Army, became a national instead of an exclusive Service, so the public may understand it better. Of late years, a good deal has been written about the Navy, which has almost become a popular subject; and the public seem to regard the naval seaman as a careless, jovial, sentimental person, who talks a strange dialect and calls his fellows by pet names. But the naval seaman is not really like that.

An ancient Admiral, one of Queen Victoria's Admirals, who not long since sailed for Port of Heaven, told the present writer that many years ago a brisk young journalist came on board the Admiral's ship, and upon being requested by the officer of the watch to state his business, announced that he proposed "to make the Navy popular";

229

whereupon he was politely shown over the side. The journalist took his revenge by writing an article in which he described the ship's guns as " rusty "; not knowing, poor lad, that they were coated with a bronze-coloured preservative.

Now that the whole tremendous business is done, memories gleam here and there out of the mist. There is the Fleet, anchored for review at Spithead, a spired street of ships narrowing out of sight. There is the same Fleet anchored in Scapa Flow on a silken sea, amid the low and desolate islands and the wheeling gulls. There is the battle-cruiser *Tiger*, shining in the rain, her scars showing where she was mended after the fight. Far away on the Pacific, sent to certain death and obeying orders, the gallant Cradock, that fine seaman and great gentleman, goes down with his ship in the darkness and storm and a flame of fire. The mine-sweeping drifters come pitching into Dover Harbour, the begrimed White Ensign flying, and the old whiskered skipper, in naval uniform, at the wheel. Out on the Atlantic, the captain of a convoying cruiser, the skin of his face drawn tight upon the bones like coloured parchment, stands upon the bridge, where he has stood for three days and three nights, and sees the huddled houses and the smoke of the port glimmering in the twilight of the dawn, with all his flock of cargo boats safe at his heels. Near land, the civilian passenger looks upon the burly figure of the destroyer captain, conning his vessel, his intent eyes, wrinkled at the corners, perpetually vigilant. By day and night, month after month, this man lives a life of concentrated attention and unrelieved responsibility, at which the civilian can but guess. . . . A motor-launch flashes by, buried in a bow-wave to her midships, a great White Ensign streaming astern, and is gone. A seaplane, descending, alights in the Sound, and a little motor-boat dashes out to tow her alongside the jetty in a seaway. Yonder is Drake's Island, past whose green slopes the English Fleet went out to fight the Spanish Armada. . . . Past and present are all of a piece, wrought of the same texture. The poet wrote, in a fine figure, that the spirits of our forefathers shall start from every wave. They need not do that. For on board every ship that carries the flag of England there are more men than ever were borne on the ship's books. They draw no rations and few see them; but when the bugle calls to clear ship for action, they are there.

THE END OF A DISPENSATION

WHEN Admiral of the Fleet Sir David Beatty hauled down his flag, the Grand Fleet was allowed to dissolve into its component parts and to vanish away, without one word of thanks from the nation's representatives, without any recognition of Sir David Beatty's services, other than his promotion to Admiral of the Fleet, which one may guess was by the King's desire. The Admiralty still delayed to grant the promised increases in pay and pension, and not a penny of prize money had been distributed. Perhaps the doing of justice to the Navy was reserved for the Peace; but it was too late. For what reason the present writer knows not, the Navy was deliberately slighted. He can but record the fact, with a regret which was shared by some millions of the public, who, as usual, found that the Government, chosen to carry their desires into execution, failed them. The effect upon the Navy itself was deplorable. It suffered under an angry sense of injury.

Some political philosophers, Mr Masefield, I think, among them, have attempted to account for the curious antagonism to the fighting services observable in this country, by assuming the existence of two kinds of temperament: the one naturally antipathetic to strife and hating the arts

of war, the other recognizing the inherent tend-
ency to violence in human nature and therefore
acknowledging, even with pride, the place of the
fighting man in the community. It may be so;
indeed, in all ages these two warring elements
have been manifest. And so, one may add, have
ingratitude, selfishness, and stupidity been manifest. These are the evils which have inspired men
with so profound a distaste for the world that they
have retreated into monasteries and hidden themselves in the wilderness. But we cannot all become
eremites. The most of us must stay in the arena
and struggle as best we may in the dust, amid the
ring of incurious faces.

The politician, who manages our affairs for us,
is as highly sensitized as a photographic plate,
which receives impressions of that which is invisible to the human eye. Thus he reproduces the
moods of the public; and thus we account for his
actions. Apparently the Government was repro-
ducing the fine shades of the sentiments of the
peaceable, who, owing to confusion of thought,
transfer their hatred of strife to the men whose
business it is to defend them from strife. You
must take the politician as he is, and admire him
for what he can do, and not perpetually gird at
him for failing to achieve what he cannot achieve.
Bear in mind that the English, whether peaceable
or warlike in theory, are the most stiff-necked
nation on earth. They will endure no man's
rule. They obey the law only because themselves
made the law. And when our statesmen are

accused of weakness, it is commonly forgotten that the exercise of their authority rests on compromise. They must persuade either the whole of the nation, or as great a part thereof as may be, that they are fulfilling the national desires, or they will be thrown aside to make room for more amenable demagogues. That is the position.

For an ignorant democracy is the reversal of government. It is no longer the first duty of a Government to govern. Its first duty is to obey. When a choice among various courses of action is presented to the Government, what determines its decision? Simply the majority. It is done by counting heads. Whether those heads entertain a wrong idea (as sometimes happens) or a right idea (as occasionally occurs) does not enter into consideration. And the whole essence of political endeavour is to turn a minority into a majority, by means of argument, persuasion, and bribery.

Mr G. K. Chesterton, who studies these things with a passionate interest, holds the comfortable belief that the democracy, in other words the majority, is by some divine decree almost invariably right. Therefore all is well. But right or wrong, the majority rules through its agent, the politician. Sometimes, of course, the politician, who is often far from clever, mistakes the minority for the majority. Then he is finished. It is quite probable, for instance, that the slight put upon the Navy by the Government was due to a mistaken estimate of the sentiment of the majority.

If that were all it would be bad enough, and sad

enough. But is it all? Was there no other, no external, influence interjected into the mechanism of British politics?

Is it not true that behind all and governing all are the International Financiers? They control all the money of the world. American, German, French, Russian, British, they are all one society. And when people ask why President This, and Mr That, and Lord the Other, did so-and-so, and why Germany escaped justice, and so forth, they find no answer. For the delegates and plenipotentiaries did, not what they would, but what they must. They dared not defy the International Financiers.

Until about twenty years ago, when Germany began to build her Fleet and to experiment with new weapons, Great Britain could have faced the situation with composure. She had a Navy fit to win the control of sea communications and keep it. There were no two navies—no half-dozen navies —elsewhere whose challenge she need fear. The submarine, the long-range torpedo, the mine, the aeroplane, the airship, poison-gas: these things were still to be. And England was immensely rich.

After the War her money was spent, and her control of the seas, in the old sense, was impaired. England can be invaded by air. Her sea entrances can be mined and made innavigable by invisible vessels. Her most powerful ships can be sunk by an invisible torpedo. Her merchant shipping can be held up or destroyed by the submarine. What is to be her future at sea? Or rather, what is the will of my lords of the high finance? They control, not only the money of the world, but the great armament firms of all nations.

In the old wars, and thence up to the date of the Fashoda affair, England, by virtue of her mastery of the seas, held the supreme power of the world, and used it to keep the peace of the world. In the Great War we beheld the might of England circumscribed, the rise of the autocracy of the International Financier, and the concurrent emergence of Bolshevism.

Under these conditions, what is to be the naval policy of Great Britain? Is it to be the maintenance of maritime supremacy as in the past? Or is it to be obedience to the International Financier, acting through the League of Nations? It is of no use to seek guidance from the politicians. They no longer lead, but follow, and they follow first of all the International Financiers. Whither they lead the people do not know, because the lords of finance work in secret. Lurking in the innermost upholstered cell of sumptuous offices in the City of London, seen and again not seen in luxurious flats in Paris, richly lodged in Berlin, nesting high in the monstrous towers of New York, flitting in and out of Vienna, inconspicuous in Budapest, pervading Constantinople, lost in Petrograd, found again in Hong-Kong: operate invisibly the members of the most powerful secret society ever known. The people of England, for the most part, are unconscious of the existence of the princes of

Mammon. They rail at the capitalist, not knowing that the capitalist exists by permission of the International Financier, and that were the capitalist to be abolished the power behind him would still control the distribution of wealth.

That power, with the composure of a god, watches the nations warring one with another, and playing with armies and navies, impoverished and starving, or momently swollen into arrogance with the illusion of riches. If England is ever to be really free, she must break that power, which is already closing about her greatest inheritance, the source of her old prosperity and her vanishing independence, the sea. Or England may make what terms she can with the princes of Mammon, and so continue to exist on sufferance. It is not a new emergency. In one form or another England throughout her history has been continually encroached upon by the alien power, and from time to time England has expelled it. Will she expel it once more, and resume her freedom, which is being bought and sold?

That is one aspect of the situation. The other aspect concerns the nature of sea warfare. The invention of aerial navigation has deprived England of a part of her advantage in the universal mode of communication, the sea. It is impossible accurately to predict the future of aerial navigation ; but it is at least certain that for many a long year water transport will continue. Therefore an island nation must first of all ensure the security of sea communications. Therefore an island nation must continue to maintain a powerful navy. That navy is required to protect the trade routes and to carry armed force to whatever point it may be needed. Hitherto, the British Navy has fulfilled that duty almost unaided.

That the Old Navy, by reason of the invention of new weapons, is disappearing as surely as the navy of wood and masts and sails vanished before steel and steam, need inspire no dismay. The evolution of weapon and of counter-weapon never stops, and what is fatal to-day may be harmless to-morrow. England must put her trust, not in machines and in weapons, but in men. They were men and not machines and weapons that won the War. The officers and men of the Navy and of the Mercantile Marine fought the War for its first two years without weapons. For the weapons they possessed they had small chance of using, and against the new weapons of the enemy they had nothing. Then, being the men they were, the seamen invented new weapons of their own, better things than the enemy could devise, bringing him to confusion. The seamen will do it again, if they are given the chance.

Before the War, the study of weapons was largely neglected by the authorities. They built enormous ships and tremendous guns, rather to the disgust of the seamen; and then occurred this curious situation : that while the politicians and the public were deluded by the mere portentous size of ships and guns, the seamen themselves, rather sulkily accepting the new engines of war, disdained to consider the potencies of mine, submarine, long-range torpedo, airship, and aeroplane.

The British Admiral is the most stubborn, loyal, honest, and indomitable creature on earth. He is bred in a tradition which decrees that war is hard fighting, and that he who can go on fighting the longer, wins. The rest, to the British Admiral, is only important in so far as it enables him to get to close quarters with the enemy and to hit him. It was this spirit which carried the Navy through the first two years of the war. It is this spirit which remains; it is the incomparable treasure of England; and all that is now necessary is to direct it to the study of modern weapons.

When ships of war were first fitted with auxiliary engines, it became a point of honour with their captains never to use those odious machines if sail could be hoisted. When the Germans employed mines and submarines, and so forth, it became a point of honour with British Admirals to make war as if these despicable engines did not exist. But when the sailing-ship captains perceived what could be done with steam, they turned to, abolished sails, and made it their business to bring the New Navy to perfection. And so, when during the War the British Admirals—not to mention some other naval officers—perceived the value of the new weapons, they set to work to evolve the New Navy, whose beginning we behold. There is now a pause. Energy is spent. There is no more enemy at sea.

But if the future is to be assured, the public must understand the situation. The collective will must enforce the just and generous treatment of the Navy, insist upon the paramount importance of a national naval policy, and see to it that the Admiralty are given full discretion to organize the New Navy. The country must continue to trust the Admiralty, because there is none else in whom to trust.

THE FUTURE NAVAL OFFICER

T HE present writer, with extraordinary presumption, has dared to conjecture that in ships and weapons the New Navy will greatly differ from the Navy of 1914; that the mine, the submarine, the aeroplane, and the airship will affect, not only the defensive position of these islands, but the whole practice of naval warfare. These developments may safely be confided to the naval officer, always provided that he is the right kind of naval officer. But if the naval officer is to be as supremely competent in the future as he has been so triumphantly first in the world in the past, a new conception of his duties must be understood and carried into execution.

The residence at the University of Cambridge of a number of sub-lieutenants was the first and hopeful sign of the change. It was the beginning of the escape from the forced and quite unnecessary exile and isolation of the naval officer from the life of the shore: from civilian society, from science, music, painting, literature and politics, from commerce and industry. The seclusion of the naval officer is, of course, the survival from the Old Navy of a custom which, like some other naval customs, has outlasted the reason for its existence. It was the theory in the Old Navy that, unless a boy was taken in childhood, he would never learn to endure the odious hardships of sea life. Very likely the original theory was fallacious; but in any case, children of twelve or thirteen were sent to sea; and there, if they did not die or run away, they remained until they were promoted to admiral's rank, or, much more frequently, until they were superannuated with the rank of lieutenant and (in default of prize money) just enough annual pension to accentuate the lack of more. But those who are acquainted with the immortal works of the admirable Marryat remember that in those easy days a half-pay spell on shore might last for months, or even years, and that a young officer found more ways than one of spending an agreeable and a prolonged holiday on the beach while receiving (such as it was) full pay from His Majesty.

The next stage was H.M.S. *Britannia*, the preparatory school of the Navy, remembered with affection by many a naval officer. Then, in the first years of the present century, arose the great educational controversy originating in the complaints of the engineer officers' branch. The dispute, which it is useless to recall, was summarily decided by Sir John (afterwards Admiral of the Fleet Lord) Fisher, who, instead of giving engineers executive rank and duties, tried to make all officers engineers. Osborne Naval College was founded in a hurry, and instead of being sent to the *Britannia*, small boys went to Osborne, which presently became a huge preparatory school, partly managed by naval officers and partly by civilians. Here they were taught a large variety of subjects, including the elements of engineering.

It should here be noted that before the new scheme, as it was called, was instituted, the late Admiral of the Fleet Sir Gerard Noel served as a member of an Admiralty Committee on the subject, and, as he told the present writer, he advised the Committee to enter boys directly from the public schools. The English public-school boy, said Sir Gerard, is good enough for us. What the Committee recommended I do not know; but if ever there was a naval officer compact of the high tradition of the Navy, it was Sir Gerard Noel; and, together with other sagacious admirals of his generation, he could see no use in the Osborne School.

One of the advantages of the public-school entry is that the boys are not nurtured from childhood in the conviction that the Royal Navy is the only institution in the visible universe worth a serious person's consideration. That he should believe it to be the finest fighting Service in the world is right. That he should unconsciously be persuaded that there is nothing else of importance is wrong, if only because that conviction prevents the young officer from doing justice to the Navy; for the effect is to divorce the Navy from the civilian life, civilian knowledge, and civilian resources upon which the Navy must ultimately depend.

The Navy has become a profession of many highly specialized branches, each of which owes its development to the achievements of science on shore. Side by side with that development, the old tradition under which the navy of masts and sails was independent of the shore, except (in the old phrase) for victuals, wood, and water, survives. There were instances during the War of extremely capable naval officers who, taken from the sea to organize the invention and appliance of some particular device urgently required, were as totally ignorant of the persons from whom to seek advice and assistance, and of the existing state of things in relation to their requirement, as if they had landed in another planet. While naval warfare, like land warfare, had become an affair of applied science, the Navy had remained aloof from civilian enterprise and unconscious of the march of events. There existed no department at the Admiralty whose business it was to study the invention and the application of modern weapons in collaboration with civilian investigators. The Navy had its own experimental establishments and these (it considered) should suffice. There was H.M.S. *Excellent*, the gunnery school on Whale Island; there was H.M.S. *Vernon*, torpedo school, an old wooden ship of the line; there was H.M.S. *Actæon*, mining school, an old wooden frigate; and so on. Within the limits to which they were restricted, the officers of these establishments did their best.

But the naval experimental establishments, compared with the great installations of private firms, were insignificant. A proportion of the most talented naval officers, whose advancement in the Service, after attaining the rank of commander, depended upon seniority, commonly left the Navy to enter private firms. Were they to remain in the Service and to obtain promotion, they would be charged with the administrative duties of a senior officer, and their particular ability would be wasted. Hence it is that the senior officers of the Navy, to whom is confided its direction, are but dimly aware of any developments in gunnery, torpedo, mining, wireless, and the like occurring since they were promoted, while the authority of the young officers who know what the Service can teach of these things, and how to use them, is strictly limited by their rank. Officially, the ability, like the authority, of an officer is estimated by the number of gold rings on his sleeve.

Moreover, in whatever the ability of an officer consists, the Service ordains that a condition of his promotion is that he puts in a certain proportion of sea-time, as it is called. Here is another survival of custom which has lost its reason; for in the sailing days the main qualification for command was, naturally, experience in seamanship. Now that many other qualifications are equally essential, an officer must spend at sea much time in which he seldom acquires any additional knowledge of seamanship whatever. There are, of course, many officers who are seamen and nothing else, and who are quite content with that noble branch of their profession. But even for the salt-horse officer, it is not necessary that he should be sent to a naval preparatory school on shore at the age of thirteen, or that he should thenceforward regard the beach and the inhabitants thereof as having been created by the Almighty in a fit of absence of mind.

In accordance with the theory that the Navy is still constantly at sea and cruising, as it used to cruise fifty years ago, for two or three years at a stretch, officers obtain a very scant allowance of leave. Although conditions have totally changed, the idea is that an officer cannot possibly be spared for longer than ten days or a fortnight without grave injury to His Majesty's Service. Hence it is that if an officer desires to improve his knowledge generally, or in particular, he must apply to go on half-pay, thereby both injuring his chances of promotion and making it almost impossible for him to defray the cost of the most modest living.

Civilians who encounter the naval officer during his brief sojourns on shore regard him with the slightly nervous admiration due to one who deals familiarly with formidable mysteries, and who is generally reputed to be able triumphantly to handle any emergency, ashore or afloat. But if the civilian ever dared to interrogate his hero in what examiners call general knowledge he would be surprised at the ensuing vacuity.

So long as the Navy was a cruising service, in whose ships guns were mounted as a matter of form, the quaint monasticism of the seaman was merely charming. To-day, when the Navy is a complex of applied sciences, when the ships are floating towns crammed with engines of destruction, and are driven by fuel which must be replenished every week or so, when they are longer in port than at sea, the extraordinary isolation of the naval officer is simply foolish. Its result, during the War, was to bring this country into extreme danger, into a peril which the public have not yet understood.

Surely it is time that the naval officer was treated like a reasonable being? If we take the analogy of the Army, we observe during the War civilians becoming generals, and commanding armies with notable success. In the Navy itself we perceive thousands of 'hostilities only' men, civilians entered straight from the shore, performing admirable service. It almost seems as if there was something in the civilian after all. Nevertheless the public are still solemnly impressed with the notion that the Navy is a great and a holy mystery, only to be apprehended by entrance in childhood, and that the practice of its craft demands the unremitting devotion of the ascetic.

As a matter of fact, this is all nonsense. There is no reason why the naval officer should become so confirmed a specialist that he knows nothing outside his own profession, and very often nothing outside his own particular branch of it. The Navy owns an unexpressed sense of injury because the public do not appreciate it. How in the world can the public appreciate what they are not allowed to know? You do not find the recluses of a monastery complaining because they are forgotten by a god-less civilization. Doctors, lawyers, and soldiers, simply because they are a part of society, do not consider that they are misunderstood by society. And why should not the naval officer be a part of society?

The traditional system of promotion in the Service should be reformed from top to bottom. An officer's age should not enter into considera-tion. Many years ago Lord Beresford suggested that the tremendous responsibilities of an admiral could seldom be properly discharged by old men. But apart from the matter of age, under the present system the senior officers speedily lose knowledge of current developments, and are re-moved from the practice of the special branch in which they are most competent. Moreover, the greater proportion of naval officers are debarred from promotion for the simple reason that there are many more junior than senior officers required at any given moment. The path to the top narrows as it ascends. Many lieutenant-commanders must retire with the rank of commander and disappear into civil life, of which they know hardly anything, with no provision save a small pension. Some of them own technical knowledge which gains them a lucrative post, but these are few. Among them are officers whom the Navy cannot afford to lose, but whose services, owing to its ridiculous system, it is obliged to forfeit. For the rest, it is merely the duty of the State to give every officer and man in its service full opportunity for fitting himself to earn a competent livelihood in the civil life to which, except in the minority of cases, he must presently return. That opportunity can never be given so long as the dissociation of the Navy from civil life is jealously maintained. The alternative is to grant a handsome pension, as in the Indian Civil Service.

The entrance of a selected number of naval officers into the universities has given to them their first acquaintance since childhood with the men and affairs of the shore. It is said that one result was that some of these young men left the Service and remained on shore. If that report was true, it shows that the Navy fails to offer sufficiently substantial advantages, and that the adequacy of the supply of naval officers in the future will depend upon reform in naval administration.

The experience of the War demolished the pleasant conviction that the Navy was wholly self-sufficing and completely organized to deal with any emergency. For, when the emergency arrived, the first thing the Navy was compelled to do was to create a new navy out of civilian material. The same thing happened to the Army, with this difference: that nobody of any intelligence imagined that the little Regular Army could fight a European war. What the Regular Army did was to sacrifice itself to gain time while the civilian army was preparing. Had the enemy fought the War at sea with any spirit, the Navy would have been obliged to do the same thing.

If preparation for war be in question, the association and interchange of naval and civilian affairs would still be essential. But the immediate need is to establish a reasonable relation between the two which shall benefit both. It is sometimes said (with an accent of despair) that reform will come, if it ever comes, from below—that is, from the Labour people. The event is highly improbable, for the more notorious demagogues manifest not the smallest interest in the matter, of which indeed they are profoundly ignorant. Nor is there any reason to imagine that the industrial and mechanical civilization of the Iron Age is likely to emit light from its lower layers, other than the angry glow of discontent.

At the same time, it is a melancholy reflection that the series of eminent politicians who have occupied the position of First Lord have never even been aware that any need for reform existed. It is true that the Sea Lords did not care to enlighten them. In the presence of these tremendous silences the present writer is conscious of what will probably be regarded as unforgivable audacity. But, after all, he did not set the yeast in the dough. It is there, and it is working.

This is a matter in which the country as a whole is concerned, for its security and its prosperity alike must still depend upon the sea services; and until a common understanding prevails between seamen and landsmen there can be no unity of purpose. Imperceptibly, the days of the exclusive Service have gone by, and the sooner the change is brought into the region of consciousness the better.

Nothing can correct the impression produced upon the mind of the landsman by some of the recent literature dealing with the life of the Navy except personal acquaintance with that Service, nor can aught persuade the naval officer that life on shore has its own intrinsic values, except becoming for a time a part of that life. The naval officer is not really the kind of person depicted in those stories about the Navy in which he is represented as a compound of profound sentimentality and romantic heroism, speaking a strange dialect, invariably addressing his friends by infantile nicknames, and romping like a child at every opportunity. This singular conception is like to misfeature the Navy as Ouida's Guardsmen, in the sumptuous Victorian Age, misrepresented the British Army. These great creatures did high credit to Ouida, and as heroes of fiction they demand homage, but they did not in fact incarnate the reality of the British Army.

The Navy enlists every variety of character, ability, and temperament, and it needs them all. But, as at present constituted, it appears that the Service itself prevents itself from giving due scope and verge to the talents with which it is endowed. In the old sailing-ship days a ferocious discipline was, fortunately, diversified by a startling indulgence. As the ships changed from creatures whose life was the will of man to monstrous mechanisms of steel, so the administration of the Service

251

became more and more mechanical. From a free company the Navy became a factory. When the man becomes the servant of the machine he is on the way to death. A mechanical system of administration kills by degrees, and presently there is nothing left but the system.